FROZEN
BLOOD

by

MICHAEL SHERIDAN

D1566519

First published in 2003 by

Mentor Books
43 Furze Road,
Sandyford Industrial Estate,
Dublin 18.
Republic of Ireland

Tel. +353 1 295 2112/3   Fax. +353 1 295 2114
e-mail: admin@mentorbooks.ie
www.mentorbooks.ie

ISBN: 1-84210-206-0

Cover by Graham Thew
Typesetting, editing, design
and layout by Mentor Books

Printed in Ireland by ColourBooks

CONTENTS

This book is dedicated to the victims
and their families who have suffered unimaginably
from the actions of brutal killers
in a society besieged by violence.

I could a tale unfold whose lightest word
Would harrow up thy soul, freeze thy young blood,
Make thy two eyes like stars start from their spheres
Thy knitted and combined locks to part,
And each particular hair to stand on end,
Like quills upon the fretful porpentine.

Hamlet

PROLOGUE

INTO THE FOREST

We never know what is waiting around the next corner. One day could start with sunshine and suddenly night could fall in a matter of a minute or an hour, long before nature decrees that to be so. Oblivion can be but a hand's distance away for the prey in the sight of the hunter. The watched can be totally unaware of the cruel stare of the stalker in the night with not even a footfall to stir a sense of danger.

In the depths of winter in a small Irish midlands town the short walk of the woman from her shop to the car, in an instant, became a fall into the abyss. From an ordinary, simple action she had been catapulted into a seemingly endless nightmare, captured by a monster thinly disguised in the shape of a human. Bound and trussed by the straps of her bra she was in the boot of a moving car being driven into a remote part of the hinterland.

Fear coursed through her veins. She screamed and kicked at the boot, to no avail. The car moved inexorably towards an unknown destination. The victim had no control and fate had deserted her. To be in this position meant one or two things, rape or death or both. She knew that she was no accidental tourist in the hands of this infernal guide.

Even in the cramped space she was thrown around like a rag doll by the speed of the car. How long it had been travelling, she could not guess. In such a situation time is frighteningly suspended. She instinctively felt that she had little time left. But she was a strong woman and would not be consigned to this man's planned destiny for her without a fight.

The first part of the horror was soon to be visited upon the terrified woman. After that there could be only one end: oblivion, merciful oblivion. But she would summon every last ounce of what would prove to be her considerable courage.

Right now, as the car moved over every bump and grind of the mountain road, her fate was in the soiled and filthy hands of a devil, a devil with rape, sexual perversion and murder on his mind. A man with such a damaged psyche that he would stop at nothing to fulfil his foul and sadistic fantasies.

His adrenalin pumped at the prospect of violating her body. Afterwards, he would get rid of her where nobody could find her. It was not just that there could be no witness to his depravity. Killing was not simply a necessity, it gave him ultimate control, his greatest kick.

The headlights of the Jeep illuminated the lonely road in front of the hunters where nothing was to be seen but the shadows of trees. It was a dark night in February and as black as it could get in the depths of the Wicklow mountains. One turn after another on a winding journey gave the same view, isolation, a view that none but the most familiar would relish. But for people who were used to it, it was part of the experience of the forbidding landscape. The driver and his companion had been there many times and it was comfortable territory. The guns they had in the back were for hunting; the men in the car had been out hunting foxes.

Out of nowhere the headlights of the Jeep illuminated a car. Then a man appeared from behind the car, opened the driver's door and sat in. The men in the Jeep recognised him and wondered what he was doing in the middle of the forest at this time of night. They saw his face as clear as daylight as he revved up his car and drove past them.

As the car sped by, the lights caught the figure of a woman running away. The hunters were mystified. What exactly was going on? One man looked at his watch – it was after 10 p.m. They got out and walked in the direction of a ditch, where they had seen the woman go.

They found her entangled in barbed wire, desperately struggling to escape. The woman became hysterical at the sight of them. There was blood all over her face and she was clearly afraid that the men were part of a gang. They calmed her down and carefully lifted her away from the wire. No, they were not with the man that had driven away. They took her to the Jeep. She told them that she had been raped and beaten. She said that the man was about to kill her when they had driven up to the spot. 'I know him,' said one of the men, remembering how his friend's sister had been groped by him in a pub.

The hunters drove out of the forest and back towards Baltinglass Garda Station in Wicklow. They knew the man: married with kids and only lived a few miles away. A bit of a loner. A bit of an oddball.

Especially around women.

Locals would later say that what happened that night was a miracle. And in a way it was.

1
A RISING TIDE

The tide of violent crime has risen inexorably in Ireland over the past decade. Murder, which once grabbed newspaper headlines, is commonplace. So too are rape, assault, robbery and gangland killing. Unprovoked attacks have become an epidemic as have violent crimes, including murder. One of the most disturbing and worrying developments is the emergence of the psychopathic killer, a species previously only achieving notoriety in the US, England and other far-off countries such as Australia and Russia.

There is an escalating feeling in Irish society of fear and vulnerability and the consequent lack of trust and isolation. Unfortunately women are increasingly targets of killers who have become, despite their psychotic natures, more adept at carrying out their heinous crimes without being brought to justice. This is an insidious development that has destroyed the quality of many families' lives. The knowledge that at any time a person can be abducted, tortured, raped and brutally murdered impoverishes and paralyses communities. The psycho killer, like a wolf, can strike at random, melt into the landscape and disappear without trace.

This killer, because he almost always has no direct link with his victims, is much more difficult to apprehend and is more often than not caught by chance rather than design. Law enforcement agencies outside this country, most particularly in the UK and the US, have been quick to realise that given the fact that these killers are hard to track down something more than conventional police work is necessary to catch them.

Since the early eighties American law enforcement agencies became increasingly aware of the emergence of an alarming phenomenon – the serial killer. While history, from Gilles De Rais to Jack the Ripper, has thrown up such killers, multiple murder had been on the upward curve from the sixties. The Boston Strangler, Albert De Salvo and Ted Bundy created fear and havoc and became media monsters in the US, while Ian Brady and the late Myra Hindley achieved the same status as perpetrators of the infamous Moors Murders.

Psychological studies and analysis became a major weapon in tracking down the killers and a mental fit became as important, and more so, than a photo-fit. This technique led to the establishment of the FBI Behavioural Science Unit at Quantico, Virginia, made famous in Thomas Harris's book and the subsequent film *Silence of the Lambs*. The men responsible for such murders, while a rare breed, share psychological traits, sexual deviation and an unusual appetite for sadism, cruelty and perversion of all kinds.

Although there are various categories of serial and psycho killers, what they have in common is a particularly cold and savage attitude toward their victims and a desire to induce terror before despatching them, mostly by stabbing or strangulation. There is also an inclination to sexual arousal through violence, rape or postmortem mutilation. They have no mercy nor do they experience remorse or guilt, rather they revel in the memory of their dastardly acts. In other words their hearts are made of ice and the liquid that courses through their veins is frozen blood.

Most murders are carried out by people who are linked in some way, be it lover, rival, husband, wife, or they may be involved in a feud or gangland activity. In some cases, like a sudden quarrel or drunken brawl, there is no premeditation: circumstances lead to an unfortunate outcome. In others there are clear motives, jealousy or revenge for some wrong, perceived or real. The psycho, or lust, killer is completely different and distinct.

Anger, lust, perversion and feelings of personal inadequacy drive him. He can be a brute with a wimpish heart or a wimp with a brutal heart. He is generally, though not always, a loner with problems dealing with the opposite sex and harbours a deep-seated hatred and distrust of women whom he will blame for all his personal and sexual inadequacies. To his core, he is cruel with an interest in pornography, in particular that category which includes bondage, sadism and torture depicting women and children suffering pain and humiliation from sexual activities.

His masturbatory fantasies will always be associated with sado-masochistic practices in which he inflicts pain and terror on his female subject whom he consigns to the status of sex slave. In his fantasies he rehearses what he will do to the unwitting victim, once he gets the opportunity. Always he is in total control; the victim will scream for mercy in the sure knowledge that he will offer none. This is a sick individual for whom, in his own mind, there is no hope of redemption and thus none for his victim.

In death, one presumes, there is no memory of pain and suffering, but the moments, the hours or days beforehand can be transformed into an eternity for the victim, an unmitigated reality of horror in which the perpetrator enjoys the role of having power over life and death. This man is relentless in pursuit of his evil objective and likes to watch and stalk his prospective victims. And when he tortures, rapes, kills and mutilates, has sexual contact with or cannibalises the corpse, he will replay the scene over and over again in his masturbatory fantasies in the same manner that ordinary men and women relive a sexual experience. The act of killing has a direct link to his twisted libido and his action has no emotional impact on him because he is an emotional bankrupt who has as little and possibly less respect for himself as he has for his victim.

The first manifestation of serial killers in Ireland was in the seventies when two Englishmen, John Shaw and Geoffrey Evans, abducted, tortured, raped and murdered two young women, Elizabeth Plunkett in Co Wicklow and Mary Duffy in Co Mayo. Their intended third victim, a nurse whom they had picked up in Co Galway, escaped and they were arrested soon after. Shaw admitted during questioning that they had intended killing one woman a week. They are still in prison. Have there been others? Patterns in other countries show that they emerge in different generations. In England Brady and Hindley were succeeded by Dennis Nilsen and later by Fred and Rosemary West.

Shaw and Evans were succeeded, in terms of conviction, in the eighties by the late and monstrous DJ, Vinnie Connell. Connell had a history of terrorising women and was convicted but then acquitted of the murder by strangulation of Patricia Furlong at the Fraughan Festival in Glencullen near the Dublin mountains. Connell had all the classical characteristics of a serial killer. Four other potential victims managed to escape with their lives.

The late nineties threw up another vicious and psychotic killer in Mark Nash who murdered his girlfriend's sister and her husband. His girlfriend was lucky to escape with her life. Nash subsequently admitted to the murder of two female Grangegorman outpatients at their house near the hospital. He later withdrew the admission. Mark Nash is not only the chief suspect but is, according to a forensic psychiatrist, by inclination, psychology, background and upbringing a very rare type of psychopathic killer, who expresses all his anger and bitterness towards his mother, whom he alleged during his trial was a prostitute, by subjecting his victims to horrendous mutilation.

In one province of Ireland, Leinster, between March 1993 and July 1998, eight women disappeared without explanation and no trace has ever been found of them. The Garda and the families of these women believe with good reason that they were abducted and murdered. Despite exhaustive investigation there have been no definite lines of inquiry.

In the preceding years three other women disappeared. Antoinette Smith went missing in early 1988 and her body was found some months later buried in bogland just off the Military Road in the Dublin Mountains. A year and a half later Patricia Doherty disappeared from the Tallaght area of Dublin two days before Christmas. Her body was found in the same area in the mountains six months later. Marie Kilmartin a thirty-six-year-old woman from Portlaoise was last seen alive at her home on December 16, 1993. Her body was found six months later in a ditch near Portarlington. All three women had been raped and strangled. The perpetrator, or perpetrators, were never brought to justice.

Over the following five years eight more women disappeared but this time without trace. This could hardly be construed as coincidence. Could the killer or killers be getting more sophisticated in the modus operandi of abduction, rape, killing and disposing of the bodies? Was a serial killer involved? A distinct new pattern of targeting and killing women had been drawn on to the map of murder in Ireland.

And this pattern when compared to similar cases in other countries is one almost exclusively utilised by serial killers.

March 26, 1993

Annie McCarrick, a beautiful American literature student in her mid-twenties, took a bus to Enniskerry, Co Wicklow. She may have taken a long walk in the woods and valleys above Powerscourt estate where one could ramble for hours without seeing another person. Later that evening she was spotted in Johnny Fox's pub in Glencullen. She was never seen again.

November 9, 1995

It was dark, just after 11.30 p.m., in the small village of Moone, Co Kildare and a young Kilkenny girl hitching home from Dublin had just been dropped at a telephone kiosk. She entered the kiosk and made a phone call. The main street was deserted.

The line clicked and, under the harsh white light that gave an unnatural glow to the kiosk, Jo Jo Dullard replaced the receiver on the cradle. The petite 5'4" girl opened the creaking door, the sound magnified by the silence.

Moments later Jo Jo Dullard stepped into a car she'd managed to flag down. She has never been seen since.

July 28, 1998

Michael and Deirdre Jacob were at their Roseberry home in Co Kildare on a sunny July afternoon. The birds were singing and the sky was clear, a day to lift the spirits. Their eighteen-year-old daughter Deirdre, with striking looks and shiny dark hair, had gone into Newbridge to post a bank draft and some letters. They were expecting her home any moment. She never arrived.

Five people saw Deirdre as she walked back home from Newbridge but not on the last 500 metre leg. In that space, she was abducted and disappeared without trace. It is unlikely that one man was responsible for the abduction, given the time of day and the location.

The Garda were slow to accept that these women were victims of a serial killer but, as a result of media attention and growing public concern, Garda Commissioner Pat Byrne set up in October 1998 a special unit named Operation Trace to re-investigate these murders and to establish if there were any links. The unit had one notable success unrelated to the other cases with the conviction in 2003 of John Crerar for the murder of Phyllis Murphy twenty-four years before but no other leads have been uncovered.

Detective Inspector Brendan McArdle, whose interest in forensic science was a vital factor in the solving of this appalling crime, is on record as saying that he believes that Crerar was not the type of killer who would stop at one murder. This view is backed up by a forensic psychiatrist who says that such a compulsive character could not resist killing again, particularly as he would have been convinced that he had got away with the 1979 murder.

These experts and others believe that Crerar has the psychological profile that would fit a suspect in the abduction and likely murders of Jo Jo Dullard and Deirdre Jacob, the latter possibly as a joint enterprise with another killer. New information given to me places Crerar's car at a disused quarry in Kildare the night after the disappearance of Jo Jo Dullard. A security guard in the nearby stables of the Aga Khan stud at the time, Crerar was a regular visitor to this quarry which has never been searched by gardaí.

In May 2001 Larry Murphy, a thirty-six-year-old father of two, was convicted of one of the most vicious kidnapping and rape incidents since the Shaw and Evans abductions, the difference being that Murphy's victim, by a piece of sheer luck, survived. But it was clear from the evidence, and the jury agreed, that his plan was to kill his victim and bury her body, and he was therefore convicted of attempted murder. The sentence of fifteen years reflects the seriousness of the crime.

But the question on the minds of the media, public and police was had Larry Murphy killed before? In the course of the trial it emerged that he carried out his kidnapping and rape with coolness and in a practised manner and was putting his victim into the boot of his car when two men on a hunting expedition disturbed him.

Murphy was a bit of a loner who lived with his wife and family in a bungalow in Baltinglass, Co Wicklow. As a carpenter he frequently travelled to building sites in and around the radius within which the three women disappeared. He also had hunting skills which took him deep into the Wicklow and Dublin mountains. In the early nineties he worked as a barman in Glencullen where

Annie McCarrick was last seen and he was working on a job in Roseberry the day before Deirdre Jacob disappeared.

It also emerged during the investigation that he raped another girl close to the spot where Jo Jo Dullard disappeared. A man with a very close resemblance to Murphy was seen arguing with John Crerar inside the gate of a disused quarry at the back of the Aga Khan stud in Co Kildare. Murphy refused to give any information to detectives about his possible involvement.

The vicious murder of teenager Raonaid Murray in 1999 had all the hallmarks of the work of an opportunistic killer who, investigating officers believe, may have killed before and will kill again. A chilling psychological profile carried out by Dr Art O'Connor and his team at the Central Mental Hospital in Dundrum, south County Dublin, shows that the man is in need of psychiatric help and is obsessed with female dominance and violence.

In the sweep of the investigation a number of apartments were raided where perverted drawings and writings depicting mutilation of the female organs were uncovered. While their alibis stood up, investigating officers had no doubt that these perverted men were also a serious threat to women.

The serial killers have left a legacy of grief to relatives of their victims, consigning them to a living nightmare for the rest of their lives. That grief is multiplied tenfold by the fact there is no resolution to the cases and the likelihood of the killer or killers being caught is remote. Could it be mere coincidence that since the conviction of Larry Murphy and John Crerar the pattern of abduction and murder has ceased?

But this type of killer is unlikely to disappear without trace and, to make sure that there will never be a carte blanche for his vile actions, it is necessary to understand where he comes from, why he is what he is and the complex and disturbing mechanism of his cruel and twisted mind.

The lineage of such killers stretches back 125 years to the Whitechapel area of East End London and to the infamous activities of Jack the Ripper. Despite millions of words written and expert investigations carried out over that century and a quarter, no one can conclusively prove the identity of the father of all serial killers. In 1888 terror struck the heart of London and the reverberations still last to this day. Replication or imitation fail to dull the effects or dispel the mystery.

Jack the Ripper, despite the incredible risks he took, ultimately left nothing to chance. But the legacy of his modus operandi, his motivation and his mind survive intact to this day. In this type of murder the passage of time simply confirms the nature and personality of the murderer and the necessity to understand him.

2
HORROR IN WHITECHAPEL

In the dilapidated, disease-ridden area of Whitechapel in London's East End in the late nineteenth century, with its run-down lodging houses, streets teeming with prostitutes and all manner of wretchedness, the cry of murder was a regular echo. Crime comes in cycles and at this time it was at the zenith of an upward curve. In 1887 there were 500 inquests into unexplained deaths in the area and in the wave of violence that followed into the next year, women seem to have been the majority of victims.

Author Tom Cullen, writing on the Ripper murders in his 1965 book *Autumn of Terror,* observed:

> In scanning the press for this period one is astounded by the number of reports of women who had been beaten or kicked to death, jumped on until they were crushed, chopped, stabbed, seamed with vitriol (sulphuric acid), eviscerated (disembowelled) or deliberately set on fire. In the preceding year thirty-five murders (seventy-six including infanticide) were recorded. Only eight convictions were secured, the majority of crimes remaining unsolved forever.

This is the background, the seething cauldron in which the mysterious killer was soon to make his terrifying mark. If the statistics suggest that either Scotland Yard or the local Metropolitan

Frozen Blood

force were incompetent, the records of the Ripper investigation prove the contrary and confirm a fact that is still true – random murder is the most difficult to solve. What happened in Whitechapel was replicated a century later to an even greater degree by the Yorkshire Ripper, who was only eventually caught because a straw was grasped by a vigilant young policeman.

The first Whitechapel victim was Mary Ann Nichols, separated from her husband for nine years 'through her drunken and immoral habits' who from time to time had been an inmate of various workhouses. She was a disorganised, alcoholic prostitute, given to wandering the streets late at night in search of business to pay for her drink and lodgings, perfect prey in the poorly lit streets and alleys of Victorian London.

She had been seen in her lodgings at 56 Flower and Dean Street at 1.40 a.m. on the morning of August 31,1888. The worse for wear from drink, she told the deputy house manager that she hadn't got the money for the rent, but to keep the bed and she would be back in a while with the money. She left and was then seen by another lodger of the same house in Whitechapel Street three-quarters of an hour later. The lodger asked her to come back but she refused and walked away as the local church bell tolled 2.30 a.m.

A half a mile away, just over an hour later, her body was found by two men on their way to work. Her throat had been cut and later in the mortuary it was established that her stomach had been mutilated, exposing her intestines. The savage death might have encouraged other prostitutes to be cautious but the drink and the lodgings had to be paid for.

Eight days later the killer struck again, upping the ante in savagery and mutilation and confirming a characteristic that has stood the test of time: once this type of killer has tasted blood, he will strike again

Annie Siffey another separated woman-turned-prostitute was seen drunk in her lodging house in the same area at 2 a.m. and, with the same problem of meeting her rent, left to do business on the street. At 6.10 a.m. on the same morning Inspector Joseph Chandler on duty in Commercial Street Station received information that another woman had been murdered. The body had been found in nearby Hanbury Street.

Chandler proceeded to the scene of the crime and found a woman lying on her back. In the words of his report, she was

> dead, left arm resting on her left breast, legs drawn up, small intestines and flap of the abdomen lying above the right shoulder, attached by a cord with the rest of the intestines inside the body, two flaps of skin from the lower abdomen lying in a large quantity of blood above the left shoulder, throat cut deeply from left and back in a jagged manner, right around the throat.

> I at once sent for Dr Phillips, divisional surgeon, and to the station for an ambulance and assistance. The doctor pronounced life extinct and stated that the woman had been dead at least two hours. The body was then removed to Whitechapel mortuary. On examining the yard, I found at the back wall of the house (at the head of the body) and about eighteen inches from the ground about six patches of blood,

varying in size from a sixpenny piece to a point and, on the wooden paling on the left of the body near the head, patches and smears of blood about fourteen inches from the ground.

The woman has been identified by Timothy Donavan, deputy of Crossinghams lodging house at 35 Dorset Street, Spitalfields, who states that he knows her about sixteen months as a prostitute and for the past four months she has lodged at the above house. At 1.45 a.m. she was in the kitchen, the worse for liquor, and eating potatoes. He [Donavan] sent to her for the money for her bed, which she said she had not got and asked him to trust her, which he declined to do. She then left stating that she would not be long gone. He saw no man in her company.

The report then gave a description of the woman, an account of the old, dirty clothes she was wearing and concluded by stating that a description of the victim had been circulated by wire to all stations. A door-to-door enquiry at all lodging houses was called for to ascertain if any suspicious character with blood on his clothing was seen after 2 a.m.

Detective Inspector Frederick Abberline in a further report established that Annie Siffey had been the widow of a coachman named Chapman from whom previously she had been separated because of her drunken habits and for some years past had been a frequenter of common lodging houses. In other words she, in common with the previous victim, was in the most vulnerable position, a perfect and easy prey for the murderer.

In the manner of succeeding generations of similar killers, the murderer had arranged the body, placing various mutilated parts in a certain pattern, making a terrifying statement and transforming his savagery into a 'work of art'. He took a great risk in a public place where he could easily have been caught in the act, in which case it would have been all over. But it wasn't. Nor was it the case that the reaction of the subsequent police investigation was inadequate. It wasn't. It was exhaustive and punctilious, as most modern cases are, but it led nowhere.

Even without the benefit of modern science and DNA the basic methodology of investigation was no different from that of today, demonstrating that every murder enquiry needs a break. Most of all, Jack the Ripper had luck on his side, far more than his pursuers would ever have, and there is nothing new in that.

The killer, in the classical sense, just sat back and waited until the next opportunity and in that run-down area, populated with needy prostitutes, opportunities came a begging. He clearly had an intimate knowledge of the ground on which he operated and probably stalked his victims whose movements were entirely predictable, so driven were they by their needs. And he most likely kept one or several rooms in the neighbourhood. Police were not thin on the ground, particularly after the first two murders, but the regularity of their work was in tune with the church clock, so he could also predict their movements. Risk, however minimised, was also part of the thrill.

In his cleverness he knew that he had to let things go quiet for a while. Whatever compulsion was driving him, he knew that instant gratification was out of the question. And given the power of masturbatory recall, he could delay until he was overwhelmed with the desire to translate the fantasy into reality. After three weeks, he could hold back no longer. In the early hours of September 30 he indulged in an orgasm of unprecedented violence.

Before that, in a letter considered genuine and posted on September 28 to The Central News Agency in London, the killer cynically became involved in the whole process that attended the murders and their aftermath, creating an extra layer of fear and loathing.

25 September 1888

Dear Boss

I keep on hearing the police have caught me but they wont fix me just yet. I have laughed when they look so clever and talk about being on the right track. That joke about Leather Apron gave me real fits. I am down on whores and I shant quit ripping them till I do get buckled. Grand work the last job was. I gave the lady no time to squeal. How can they catch me now. I love my work and want to start again. You will soon hear of me with my funny little games. I saved some of the proper red stuff in a ginger beer bottle over the last job to write with but it went thick like glue and I cant use it. Red ink is fit enough I hope ha.ha. The next job I do, I shall clip the ladys ears off and send to the police officers just for jolly wouldn't you. Keep this letter back till I do a bit more work then give it out straight. My knife's so nice and sharp I want to get to work right away if I get a chance. Good luck.

> Yours truly
> Jack the Ripper

Don't mind me giving the trade name.

At right angles to the rest of the letter:

> PS Wasnt good enough to post this before I got all the red ink off my hands curse it.
> No luck yet. They say I'm a doctor now. ha ha.

The night after he posted the letter, he struck again with a vengeance, killing two prostitutes in one night. This provided clear evidence of the role of risk-taking in his compulsion. The first victim was Elizabeth Stride, forty-five years of age and known locally as Long Liz, the second Catherine Eddowes, two years younger but ravaged by the effects of alcohol and poor diet. But the proximity in time and place indicated that the Ripper despite his compulsion was, like any good bookmaker, fastidious about minimising the risk of being caught.

In the first case Stride was attacked in a narrow court in a quiet thoroughfare, which after midnight would have been pitch black. A man from a nearby social club stumbled across the body at 1 a.m. He alerted the police and ten minutes later two doctors arrived for an on-the-scene examination. They noted that the body was lying on the left side, left arm extended from the elbow and in the clenched hand some sweets. The legs were drawn up, not in a natural falling position, but by the killer. The body was still warm and the throat was deeply gashed.

At around the same time that the murder was taking place, Catherine Eddowes was in police custody, arrested earlier in the evening for being drunk. Having been adjudged sober she was released at 1 a.m. Just forty-five minutes later a constable on patrol found the body of a woman in Mitre Square. Her face was mutilated almost beyond recognition. A portion of her nose was cut off and the lobe of the right ear nearly severed. Her throat was cut and she had been disembowelled. Just fifteen minutes earlier the constable had patrolled the same spot where the body was found, and noticed nothing untoward. An eyewitness had seen a man talking to a woman nearby just five minutes after the constable had passed on his patrol. It was dark and he could not positively identify either party. But it was hardly a coincidence, meaning the Ripper had just ten minutes to do the dastardly deed.

The postmortem examination revealed that the left kidney and uterus were missing. In the immediate follow-up investigation a constable discovered at the bottom of a stairwell a bloodstained apron which later matched a missing piece from the victim's clothing. On the wall of the stairwell he saw a cryptic message written in chalk.

> The Juwes are the men who will not be blamed for
> nothing.

Jews was deliberately misspelt but the audacity of the act was obvious – to leave clues that would taunt the police, public and the local Jewish population. It also had the desired effect of further terrorising the community and mocking the investigation. There was more to come.

The Central News Agency received a postcard the day after the double murder. There is some dispute whether it was posted on September 30, giving information which only the killer could have known, or October 1 when details of the murder became general knowledge. But in the light of the last two lines which are direct references to the first letter it can be considered authentic.

> I was not codding dear old Boss when I gave you the tip, you'll hear about saucy Jacky's work tomorrow double event this time number one squealed a bit couldn't finish straight off. Had not got time to get ears for police. thanks for keeping last letter back till I got to work again,
>
> Jack the Ripper

Rewards for information leading to the arrest of the killer were offered by the police, the local MP, Mr Montagu, and a vigilance committee headed by George Lusk of Mile End Road. Lusk's name would be indelibly linked to the Ripper's most bizarre acts, not as a result of anything he did or did not do himself but by the killer's new-found desire to publicise his evil doing in the most foul of manners.

On October 18 Lusk brought a parcel that had been addressed to him to Leman Street Police Station. The parcel contained what was subsequently confirmed to be a portion of a human kidney and a letter which read as follows:

From hell.

Mr Lusk,

Sir

I send you half the Kidne I took from one women prasarved it for you tother piece I fried and ate it was very nise. I may send you the bloody knif that took it out if you only wate a whil longer.

Signed   Catch me when You can Mishter Lusk

Like the message on the stairwell the misspellings are considered by experts to be deliberate. The immediate impression given is that the killer is from a working-class background and semi-literate. The writer does not attach his trademark name to the bottom as in the other communications and this letter differs from them in tone and shape. So was it the third authentic communication from the Ripper or just another of the many false letters purporting to be the killer from cranks, the disaffected or the simply weird?

The answer was found in the analysis of the kidney portion sent to Lusk. The pathological examination was carried out by Dr Openshaw of the London Hospital Museum. He found it was the kidney of a middle-aged woman and had been removed in the previous three weeks. It was in an advanced state of Bright's disease, which is a chronic inflammation of the kidneys. All these findings tallied with Catherine Eddowes whose remaining kidney was in this exact state and contained two inches of renal artery. There was one inch on the posted kidney, the exact length of the portion missing.

This removed any doubt about the identity of the letter-writer.

Signed or not it was sent by Jack the Ripper whose Jekyll and Hyde character could easily account for the change of tone and spelling in the letter. He also wanted to sow the same confusion among the public that raged in his own mind, evidence of a warped intelligence.

The 'catch me if you can' sentiment is not simply arrogance but also a real invitation. The experience of succeeding generations of such killers shows that they have a real difficulty in dealing with their compulsion and many expressed a sense of relief when eventually caught. The accompanying high got from killing was followed by a low as is characteristic of the manic personality.

In another era with the benefits of huge improvements in forensic science that missive with the accompanying evidence could have resulted in the capture and conviction of Jack the Ripper. But in the shadowy gas-lit streets of Whitechapel in the 1880s the only way was by chance or mistake. This psychotic butcher had luck on his side, but also the sure knowledge that the more he killed the greater the likelihood that his luck would one day run out.

Catherine Eddowes was the accepted penultimate killing of Jack the Ripper's career and for over a century writers and experts from a number of fields have speculated about the identity of the killer and tried to offer explanations why, after the next murder, the killing stopped so suddenly. Millions of words have been written about the killer and the contemporary best-selling crime novelist Patricia Cornwell spent millions of dollars in her efforts to track down and identify the world's most famous serial killer.

Ten days after the double murder the Ripper struck for the last time but in the most horrific fashion, as captured in the headline of the *Illustrated Police News:*

ANOTHER WHITECHAPEL HORROR,
MORE REVOLTING MUTILATION THAN EVER

A landlord's collector Thomas Bowyer was sent to a dilapidated lodging house at Miller's Court, Dorset Street in Spitalfields on the morning of November 9 to collect rent. Having knocked on the door of number 13 and getting no reply, he looked through the window which was broken. He caught sight of the bloodstained body of a prostitute he knew as Mary Jane. He returned with the landlord who dispatched him to Commercial Street Police Station.

Mary Jane Kelly was of Irish extraction and had at one time lived in Wales where her husband had died in a mine explosion. According to witness statements she had been living with a man, Joe Barnett, but he had left her, possibly as a result of her alcoholism.

When the police arrived they were confronted with a scene of shocking butchery, as if the Ripper had lost every last vestige of self-control. Perhaps it was the fact that the murder was the only one committed indoors and there was more time and less chance of being caught.

The room was tiny, serving to amplify the ghastly sight that confronted the investigators. Kelly's throat was cut so deeply that she had almost been decapitated, the bed and sheets saturated with blood. Her face was mutilated so badly that all that was left was an open sore. Her nose and both breasts were cut away and placed on the bedside table along with pieces of flesh cut from her thighs. Her stomach had been ripped open and her uterus and liver cut out. The uterus was missing but the liver had been placed between her feet. Her legs had been placed wide apart, a mass of gore between them and her left hand had been placed into her intestines.

In the fireplace there were some burnt remnants of the victim's clothing which had provided the necessary light for the Ripper's work, his shadow cast over the grimy walls as he completed his ghastly handiwork. He then, as usual, disappeared into the night. What was unusual was that it was his last act of murder as far as we know but certainly in the Whitechapel area. Was he intelligent enough to realise that his streak of good luck would run out the more chances he took?

This is not what some theorists believe. They believe the compulsion to kill would be too strong to simply stop. Later serial killers such as Peter Sutcliffe, the Yorkshire Ripper, and Dennis Nilsen, the homosexual killer, were unable to stop. They had to keep going until they were caught. So the theorists proposed that the killer ended up in a lunatic asylum, died or fled to another country.

The identity of the Ripper has been pored over, with succeeding generations of writers and experts pointing the finger at, among others, royalty, a barber, a doctor and an artist. Stephen Knight stumbled closest to the truth as far back as 1975 in *Jack the Ripper: The Final Solution*. He pointed the finger at the famous artist Walter Sickert. However he considerably diluted his finding by positing that the murders were carried out as a Masonic conspiracy involving others, including a famous physician Sir William Gull and a cab driver named Nettles.

But his theory about Sickert's involvement, based mainly on an interview with the artist's son, came closer to cracking the case than any previous writer and his suspicion concurs with Patricia Cornwell's findings in her book *Portrait of a Killer: Jack the Ripper – Case Closed*. She had the advantage over Knight in the use of her vast financial resources and the help of modern forensic techniques, which, she claims, exposes Sickert as the author of the Ripper letters.

Cornwell maintains that Sickert's paintings show that the artist continually depicted his horrific mutilation of the victims. Sickert's paintings of prostitutes are attendant with all the squalor evident in the lives of the real victims and the Camden Town Murder series, where he painted scenes of violence and murder, also reveal Sickert's obsession with true crime.

In circumstantial terms Sickert worked and lived in the area of the murders where he also kept several rooms and used prostitutes as models for his paintings. It is more than likely that local prostitutes might have known him and had nothing to fear on encountering him. But he would have been, as a once-aspiring actor, a master of disguise – if he needed to hide his identity.

Ripper author Stephen Knight was shown a bag containing surgical instruments which was inexplicably among the belongings left by the artist. Knight also points to the only credible eyewitness account placing a man with one of the victims. The description perfectly fitted Sickert who was twenty-eight at the time of the killings. This is, according to experts, the optimum age for psychotic killers and, psychologically, Sickert was a misanthrope and suffered from bouts of depression which caused him to withdraw from social contact for long periods of time. He was also described by a close friend as having a Jekyll and Hyde character. This fits the profile of such killers who are generally by their nature, loners.

In forensic terms Cornwell completes the picture by proving that two Sickert letters and two Ripper letters came from the same batch of Gurney Ivory laid paper. Further, the match between the short edge cuts on the four identified sheets shows they came from the same quire (twenty-four sheets) of paper.

Compelling enough evidence but even so doubts will always remain about the true identity and motivation of Jack the Ripper. He was and still remains in the top echelon of sexual psychopaths whose pathological hatred of women and sexual deviancy led him to inflict appalling violence and postmortem mutilation on his victims.

3
SLAUGHTER IN KANSAS

'In cold blood' is a phrase that describes killing in which there is no emotion involved on the part of the perpetrator. There is no passion, no anger, no revenge, no feeling at all of either mercy or remorse. It is as if the killer turns off in the act, all feeling is switched off like the lights of a house last thing at night and the blood coursing through the veins is suddenly frozen separating all thought from feeling. In the dark cavern of this secluded world he is immune to his own savagery. It seems as right, and matters as little, to kill a human being as to squash a fly or a bug.

There is a mental eclipse that disassociates the killer from both the act and the victim as if he has stepped outside himself and is looking on dispassionately at the dramatic play he acts out and in which the victim is but a shadow. It is hard to believe that Jack the Ripper could kill and mutilate and defile his victims with such abandon and lack of feeling, and feed icily on such hideous demise. Yet it is true, if not quite the whole truth; something else must have led to that point of separation between thinking and feeling.

Tracking down such killers is hugely difficult, often leaving investigators open to unjustified criticism. Something extra is needed on top of the conventional investigative techniques, and that is analysing the killer's actions, building a profile that fits not his face but his mind, background and behaviour. It is a technique, like the tracking of missing persons, underdeveloped and underused in

Ireland.

In the US it has been utilised for over four decades and in England close to three and has become, like many detection techniques as close to a science as can be possible with matters of the mind. The experts are dealing with people whose emotions are cross-wired in distorted minds through which abominable thoughts flow in abysmally cruel directions. Those minds, thoughts and emotions need to be thoroughly analysed if greater and more dreadful crimes are to be solved and prevented.

Such minds have operated in this country and, in the past decade, regretfully more successfully than their counterparts in other countries. These killers, in an alarming number of cases, have left no traces behind. The bodies, the greatest repository of evidence, have been successfully hidden giving the family of the victims no hope of resolution. Other killers have been caught but the lessons of their activities have not, for a variety of reasons, been successfully learnt. Their histories deserve examination as do those of killers from other countries for the simple reason, how else do we learn but by experience. In this exploration of the minds and inclination of killers, one more historical example is apposite.

The location could not have been in greater contrast to the teeming, run-down hovels of Whitechapel in late nineteenth-century London. The sparsely populated settlement of Holcomb nestled in the wheat plains of western Kansas, seventy miles east of the Colorado border set in flat lands that stretch forever towards the horizon. It was a small farming community in which horses and cattle were more numerous than the prostitutes of East London. It was seventy-one years later – mid-November 1959.

Until this time, nobody in Kansas, not to mind America, had ever heard of Holcomb, a small sleepy town with under 300 inhabitants. These were for the most part decent, hard-working, church-going folk used to the low-key dramatic rhythm of life: birth, marriage and death and other natural expectations – deliverance from hardship and future prosperity. But a ghastly happening was to spread the name of Holcomb all over the continent.

The night of November 14 was clear and the countryside was amply and beautifully lit by the moon. There was little or no wind so there was hardly a rustle in the trees and a tranquil atmosphere pervaded River Valley Farm, which lay seven miles outside Holcomb. The two-storey fourteen-roomed white-fronted house rose like a sentinel, even more visually impressive under the moonlight.

Inside prosperous forty-eight-year-old farmer, Herb Clutter, his wife Bonnie and their teenage children, son Kenyon and daughter Nancy, were asleep in their separate bedrooms. Bonnie was a semi-invalid and had her own room upstairs on the same floor as her children. Herb slept in the master bedroom on the ground floor of the house.

Just after midnight a car turned into the tree-lined avenue and a minute later pulled to a halt under a tree opposite the house. The occupants, two ex-cons and drifters, had robbery on their minds and had a knife, a shotgun and a roll of tape to carry it out. After a brief argument about carrying out the crime they got out of the car and walked to the back door of the house which was unlocked. There had never been a reason for this family to fear anything.

One of the men had been informed by a fellow con, who had worked at one stage on the farm, that there was a safe in the house. It was obvious from the house and the surroundings that the Clutters were a relatively wealthy family. What the informant did not know was that Herb, a fastidious man, never carried or kept cash.

The back door led them into an office and with the help of a flashlight they searched it but there was no sign of a safe. They moved into the hallway and stopped in front of a door. Pushing it open they woke Herb Clutter. They took him, dressed in his pyjamas, into the office and asked him to point out the safe. He told them, truthfully, that there was none there or anywhere in the house. One of the intruders then ripped out the telephone wire in the office and another one in the nearby kitchen. As he returned to the office he heard a noise from upstairs.

The other man had taken the only cash in a billfold from the farmer – thirty dollars. The two then brought him up the stairs and they entered Bonnie's bedroom. Herb turned on the light and reassured his wife that she would come to no harm, the men just wanted money. She began to cry and emptied her purse which contained a few dollars. The men then went to Kenyon and Nancy's rooms, took them out and locked them in the bathroom. They scoured their rooms and found nothing but a silver dollar and a transistor radio.

One of the men took this pathetic booty with the addition of a pair of binoculars and went outside to store them in the car. He returned to the house and with the help of his accomplice tied up Herb Clutter and brought him to the basement. There they trussed him up with more rope and laid him on a cardboard box. Kenyon was then taken downstairs to a playroom and similarly trussed up with the rope around his neck so that if he tried to escape he would choke. Bonnie and Nancy were tied up and left in their bedrooms.

After again looking for the safe they went back upstairs and placed tape around Bonnie's mouth and face. For some reason they did not do the same to Nancy. One, Dick Hickock, wanted to rape her but his accomplice Perry Smith, in a moment of what turned out to be twisted morality, would not allow the girl to be interfered with sexually.

They returned downstairs and taped Herb and Kenyon. Everywhere they went in the house one man turned out the lights and they continued their journey by aid of the flashlight. They were now faced with leaving the scene of the crime with four witnesses and a possible ten-year sentence if they were caught. But there was something more to these two than pragmatism and self-interest. Ice ran through their veins; their emotions, their thoughts, their inhibitions and most of all mercy was frozen over.

Perry Smith cut Herb's throat with the knife and when he began to struggle from the ropes, took up the shotgun and blew his brains out. The fusillade reverberated all over the house. Kenyon was next and after both were dead, the men scrambled about the floor retrieving the cartridges. God only knows what was going through the minds of Bonnie and Nancy at this moment.

Nancy screamed for mercy as they walked through her bedroom door. She got none and turned her head away as the bullet blasted out of the barrel and scattered the teenager's brains and blood all over the wall and ceiling above her bed. Bonnie was last. And then the men left with the used cartridges and forty dollars.

Some months later the perpetrators were arrested and five and a half years later, on April 14, 1965, Dick Hickock and Perry Smith were hanged one after the other for the merciless slaughter of the Clutter family. The effects of the murders on the community, the area and the country at large were controversially but superbly chronicled in Truman Capote's classic novel *In Cold Blood*.

As with the Ripper, the murders and motivation of the killers were examined minutely but more pertinently psychiatrists had the opportunity to interview the killers and compare notes from interviews with similar seemingly merciless individuals. While the initial motive for the River Valley Farm murders was robbery and secondarily the elimination of witnesses to that robbery, the savagery of the act for such little monetary return required better explanation. For example, the needless terror and fear instilled in the victims and the almost ritualistic trussing and positioning of the victims in advance of the actual killings. But, like the Ripper whose victims had done him no harm, there was some kind of warped reckoning.

Smith, the more intelligent and reflective of the two who had carried out the killings, explained it somewhat during his confession referring at first to Herb:

> I didn't want to harm the man. I thought he was a very nice gentleman. Soft spoken. I thought so right up to the moment I cut his throat. They [the Clutters] never hurt me. Like other people. Like people have all my life. Maybe it's just that the Clutters were the ones who had to pay for it.

But what a price Smith exacted for the real and perceived wrongs he had been subjected to in his life and if he could adjudge the Clutter family as decent people why could he not differentiate between them and the real wrongdoers? One moment he considers Herb Clutter a very nice and gentle person and the next instant he is cutting his throat. It does not make a lot of sense unless in the interim Smith superimposed another monstrous image on his victim thereby suspending his initial feelings.

The deliberate nature of Smith and Hickock's actions up to the point of the killings gives no indication of insanity or evidence that at the time they could not differentiate between right and wrong. In fact right to the moment they took the decision to wipe out the Clutter family, they showed remarkable coolness and sense of purpose, from the entry to the house to the tying up of the family and the cutting of phone lines, and afterwards in the punctilious collection of the used cartridges.

So what happened in between? For the purposes of the trial a psychiatric evaluation was carried out by Dr Mitchell Jones of the State Hospital in Topeka, Kansas. Almost all his findings were inadmissable in evidence. The McNaughten Rules limited his evaluation to the question of whether the defendants could distinguish between the right and wrong of what they were doing at the time of the murders: a simple yes or no situation.

What Dr Jones did spot in Hickock and Smith were a number of traits, which he could not evaluate in context since this was a most unusual event at the time. But his observations could be applied some years later to the basic psychology of serial killers, observations that could go some way to explain what possessed the men, and in particular Smith, to indulge in an orgy of violence.

His main findings in Hickock's case were:

- Above-average intelligence.
- No sign of mental confusion.
- Signs of emotional abnormality – he knew what he was doing and yet went ahead.
- Impulsive – does things without thought of consequences or future discomfort to himself or others.
- Incapable of learning from experience.
- Very low self-esteem, secretly feels inferior to others and sexually inadequate.
- Uncomfortable with other people. Unable to form and hold enduring personal attachments.

In Smith's case:

- Above-average intelligence.
- Paranoid orientation towards the world. Suspicious and distrustful of people whom he thinks are unfair to him.
- Poor ability to separate real situations from his own mental projections – all people are hypocritical, hostile and deserving of what he can do to them.
- Has an ever-present, poorly controlled rage, easily triggered which can lead to violence.
- Unable to control the mounting rage. When that rage is not directed at others, it is towards himself, resulting in suicidal thoughts.
- Poor ability to organise thinking. Gets lost in detail and drifts away from reality.

- Very few close emotional relationships with other people.
- Little feelings for others and attaches little value to human life.

Dr Joseph Satten of the Meninger Clinic, a pioneer in the study of murders without apparent motive, consulted with Dr Jones and agreed with his evaluation of Hickock and Smith. He concluded that Hickock was peripheral and the act was essentially that of Smith who matched the profile of other killers whom he had both interviewed and evaluated.

In a collaboration with three colleagues Dr Satten, in an article published in *The American Journal of Psychiatry*, explored the mind of a murderer who kills without any apparent motive. The authors had examined four men convicted of seemingly unmotivated murders. The men had been found sane before their trials but further psychiatric examination was recommended.

A simple question was to be answered: how could a person as sane as this man commit an act as crazy as the one for which he had been convicted? The four criminals included a soldier, who had mutilated and dismembered a prostitute; a labourer, who had strangled a fourteen-year-old boy who had rejected his sexual advances; an army corporal, who bludgeoned to death another young boy because he thought he was being made fun of; and a hospital employee who drowned a girl of nine by holding her head under water.

Dr Satten noted that guilt and remorse were strikingly absent and that people and victims were scarcely real to them. When such senseless murders occur, they seem to be an end result of increasing tension and disorganisation in the murderer, which has started before ever coming into contact with the victim. By fitting the unconscious conflicts of the murderer, the victim unwittingly serves to set in motion his homicidal potential.

These killers perceive innocuous and relatively unknown victims as provocative and suitable targets for aggression. There does not have to be a reason other than their own heightened tension and lack of control. At such times the target of their aggression loses any real meaning and the impulse to murder takes over. Death and destruction is the inevitable result of the compulsion.

Dr Satten concluded that Smith fitted this profile because of both his background and his actions. He also pointed out that three of the murders, Nancy, Kenyon and Bonnie, were logically motivated because Herb had already been killed but it was the first murder that mattered psychologically. Herb at the point of being shot was, in Smith's mind, a key figure in his traumatic past. This is who he was destroying, not the owner of River Valley Farm. And, in classical serial-killing experience, once the first murder had been committed, the rest were a matter of course.

The postmortem photographs of the Ripper victims, with the exception of Mary Kelly, with a strange sense of irony express repose and a peace that they never had in life. Whatever the level of cosmetic applied, and it could not have been too sophisticated at that time, their expressions communicate a release both from their horrendous deaths and awful existence. They had been living lives of unremitting and intense desperation and in death they attained a certain dignity which had been denied them even in their last moments.

Not so with the victims of the River Valley Farm slaughter. Their lives had been exemplary, bright and awash with expectation, possibly with the exception of Bonnie, who was afflicted with psychosomatic frailty and illness. Herb was in the prime of his life and the full of his health, he had just had a medical for an insurance policy and was adjudged fit as a fiddle. He was a big, hardworking man but gentle in every respect. At sixteen Nancy was going to go to college, had a nice boyfriend and was full of the anticipated joys of her future. Kenyon, a year younger, a tall, innocent young man, already had excellent handiwork skills.

There were two other family members, living away, Eveanna, married and mother of a ten-month-old child, and Beverly, training to be a nurse and engaged to be married. The invitations to the wedding scheduled for Christmas week had been printed. The Clutters had everything to live for – had they been allowed. The postmortem photographs, a freeze-frame of their demise, show how in death they were robbed of all dignity.

Such killers, as years of study has proved, see the world only through their own eyes. The only people they feel sorry for is themselves and they are by nature compulsive liars. Perry Smith's final piece of self-delusion was left for the gallows. His last words were:

> It would be meaningless to apologise for what I did.
> Even inappropriate. But I do. I apologise.

Too little. Too late

4
DEVIL'S ENVOYS

There was a picture on the front page of *The Irish Times*. Four well-built gardaí were wading out from the sea towards the shore. Between them they were carrying what appeared to be a blanket. It was an unusual photograph for the time. On the surface it wasn't disturbing because the expressions of the gardaí did not betray the import of what they were doing. Clearly there was something under the blanket, hence the necessity for four strong men.

There was a hidden horror. A body lay under the blanket: a young girl on whom chance had played a ghastly and abominable trick. The policemen carrying the body were emerging from the sea at Duncormack on the south Wexford coast.

It was a weekend at the end of August 1976 and the sunny weather had prompted many young Dubliners out of the metropolis in search of fun. The east coast was popular for such breaks and in particular Brittas Bay which was just over an hour's drive and boasted a long, lovely beach, sand dunes and a number of lively pubs. It was also cheap and cheerful with caravan parks the main provider of accommodation.

The atmosphere with the background of the rolling waves of the Irish sea was conducive to good humour. There was rarely any trouble other than the intermittent drunken row or domestic flare-up.

Among the crowds that Saturday night, August 28, was a group of five Dubliners who had travelled by car and intended staying in a caravan belonging to a friend. There was a problem about the key and while it was being sorted out they went to McDaniel's pub where the clientele was largely young, loud and very happy. Two of the group looked particularly happy. Elizabeth Plunkett, a twenty-three-year-old from Ringsend, and her boyfriend's sister Mella Bushe who had just returned from a holiday in the south of France.

They sported the typical tan from the Cote D'Azur, a deep chestnut brown colour that literally glowed and enhanced all their most attractive qualities. It would have made them stand out from the hundreds of other holiday makers that thronged the barn-like pub.

It should have been a great night for the five young Dubliners: the pub was heaving, the night was young and the drink was flowing. But there was a glitch. Elizabeth Plunkett had a difference of opinion with her boyfriend Damien Bushe which turned into a row. It reached a head and sometime after 10.30 p.m. Elizabeth announced that she was going back to Dublin and walked out of the pub.

Her friends followed but she would not be persuaded to return to McDaniels. Her annoyance, perhaps intensified by drink and the natural headstrong pride of youth, drove the young woman away. She kept on walking. Her friends returned to the pub, presuming that she would come back when she had cooled down. Unfortunately that was not to be.

Elizabeth walked on into the darkness that enveloped her and straight into a trap laid by two sexual vampires. The trap was laid, not for her, specifically, but the tiny incidence of a minor row led her, by coincidence, into the lair. She must have seemed like a vision, as the headlights of the car illuminated her from behind. Evil sometimes gets all the breaks.

Earlier in the evening two Englishmen in their early thirties had been drinking in another pub in Brittas Bay, Jack White's. They, like Hickock and Smith, were drifters with a particularly dangerous pedigree. They had just been released from Mountjoy Prison after serving, under assumed names, eighteen months of a two-year sentence for burglary. But that was only the tip of the criminal iceberg. Their names were Geoffrey Evans and John Shaw.

They had a string of convictions and had spent most of their lives in and out of jail. Both had been married but were now separated. They were also sexual deviants. One had a conviction for rape and sexual assault. Before they arrived in Ireland they were the prime suspects for the rape of three young girls in England. They were a deadly duo and the danger they presented was all the more potent because of the rudderless nature of their lives. They were living on their wits and the psychotic nature of their minds was reaching its peak.

Part of their discussions in Jack White's pub concerned the robbery of caravans in the area but they were also on the lookout for women to rape. They left the pub and drove down the dark roads after the turn off to Brittas Bay. Some time later they passed a young woman walking along the road. They drove on and Shaw got out of the car so that the potential victim would not be intimidated by the presence of two men. Evans then offered the woman a lift. Elizabeth Plunkett got into the car. Shaw was picked up along the road and got in the back seat. Her fate was sealed.

They drove to the entrance of a wood. They then began to beat their helpless victim and dragged her out of the car. On and on they pulled her, over a barbed wire fence, into the darkest recesses of the wood where, in safety, their perverted fantasies could be fulfilled. Elizabeth Plunkett was repeatedly raped by both men.

Despite the ferocity of the killing of the Clutter family, the perpetrators had shown some small level of mercy – the end for their victims was quick. Perry Smith for all his blood-letting had spared the teenage daughter Nancy the attentions of his companion Dick Hickock's perverted sexual desires. Smith's mixed-up morality, condoned killing but absolutely ruled out rape.

In the Wicklow wood that night no such niceties of psychotic behaviour existed. As the hours passed the victim was subjected to merciless mental and physical torture. Rape for these monsters was not simply about sexual gratification but more about control and inflicting extreme pain.

During the night Shaw left to move the car so that it would not bring attention to them. While he was away, Evans dozed off and the shattered victim made a desperate effort to escape. She dragged her wounded body through the undergrowth to the barbed wire perimeter fence. In her desperation she became entangled in the wire and had not the strength to extricate herself. Her agony was complete when she heard the footsteps of Shaw returning. He dragged her away from the fence and back into the woods.

The men had fled England because, if caught, their victims would have identified them. In this appalling act, they had gone further than before. Evans determined that Elizabeth Plunkett would have to be killed and ordered Shaw to carry out the act. As dawn approached she was strangled.

The killers had no thought for the mangled and defiled woman. Utmost in their minds was self-preservation and how they could buy time by disposing of the body so that it would not be found for a long time, if ever. This was no easy task given the circumstances of the murder, its location and the fact that friends and family of the victim would be alarmed by her disappearance. But just as luck had deserted the victim, it was on the side of the perpetrators. The sea was nearby and the most obvious destination for the body. Later on Sunday night after burgling a number of caravans in the vicinity, they loaded the body into the boot of the car and drove to one of the caravan parks.

They stole a lawnmower to act as an anchor and took it and the body to a boat moored nearby. They rowed out into the sea as far as they could, weighted the body with the lawnmower and heaved it overboard into the waters of the Irish Sea. As Elizabeth Plunkett's family and friends searched frantically for her just a few miles away, her mortal remains sank into the depths of the ocean. The killers returned to the shore.

While burning the victim's clothing in a caravan park, a local garda came across them and asked them what business they had there. After lying and giving false names, they were asked to move on, as they were not residents of the park. They did so, rapidly, much relieved that their lying had seemingly worked. But such small encounters can lead to bigger things.

After being released from prison, they had stayed with an English friend in Fethard, Co Tipperary, and that is where they returned the following day, Monday, the same day that the victim's family reported her missing. The drifters and rapists, now elevated to the status of murderers, borrowed a car and took to the road. They committed a series of burglaries, taking the precaution of stealing registration plates to replace their own.

The pair eventually ended up in Galway where, some miles outside the city in Barna, they bought a mobile home, which they used as a base and storage facility for another spate of robberies. They also stole a car and fitted it with new tyres and registration plates. These men were masters of their trade and in every way as inventive as their Kansas counterparts. More pertinently, they had tasted blood and got away with murder, which provides great impetus and encouragement for such men to kill again. Elizabeth Plunkett had faded from their consciousness. Their thoughts were firmly fixed on the opportunity of preying on the next victim.

And, in a sense, they could not have picked a better place than the beautiful setting of Connemara where, miles from the busy thoroughfares of town, a myriad of boreens lead to many isolated mountain and lakeside locations. It was perfect countryside for the pursuit of victims and the disposal of bodies.

But the countryside, despite being ideal for their vile intentions, also had the potential to spring the very trap they had planned for their victims. In the US or England a larger geographical area allows serial killers to operate from State to State and county to county and then disappear into large populations of people, but this was not the case in Connemara. The further they moved into the sparsely populated part of rural Ireland, the more they would stand out. A stranger becomes very obvious in a small town unless operating under the cover of darkness.

Although subsequently called into question and disbanded after the Kerry Babies case, at this time there was a highly experienced and accomplished group of investigators of serious crime known under the collective title of the Murder Squad. Already the investigation into the disappearance of Elizabeth Plunkett was underway. A sandal belonging to the victim was found in the wood in Wicklow. The local police called in the Murder Squad and members of the squad went to the scene.

Another item was found which linked the men questioned in the caravan park to the scene of the crime and an all-country station alert was put out for the men. Meanwhile a shopkeeper in Maam in the heart of Connemara served petrol to the two drifters. He was struck by the terse and unfriendly attitude of the man who got out of the car. Most tourists or visitors would engage in small talk about the weather or any of the most trivial subjects. Not this one. If Shaw or Evans knew anything about human behaviour they would have realised that this distant and unengaging attitude would have the opposite effect to that intended. It would, in an isolated rural community used to friendliness and small talk with strangers, draw attention to them.

As they drove off, the shopkeeper made a mental note of what they looked like and scribbled down the registration number of the car. The following morning he rang the gardaí and recounted the details which might have seemed of no consequence.

The drifters drove on always with eyes on the road for another potential victim and late that evening arrived in Castlebar, Co Mayo. It was September 22, 1976. There they spotted a young woman alone in a telephone kiosk. As with Elizabeth Plunkett, they stopped and waited, like two foxes quietly circling a lamb. With an uncanny foretaste of what would happen almost two decades later, a young woman would walk from a lonely kiosk into the arms of death.

Although it was a chance encounter, it was part of a greater plan laid by the two monsters. They intended to abduct, rape and murder one young woman a week. The girl came out of the kiosk and Shaw followed her. He jumped on her, bringing her to the ground, while Evans gunned the car right beside the struggling pair. The girl was beaten and dragged into the back seat. They drove away. The girl was repeatedly raped by both men as they swopped places in the driver's seat. For over sixty miles this continued until the pair pulled in to a remote spot, the old railway station at Ballinahinch. The rape and abuse continued and the girl was tied to a tree.

People later told of hearing cries of agony but thought it was the suffering of a wounded or trapped wild animal. But it was a woman being subjected to a litany of depraved torture, literally suffering the agonies of the damned. Shaw and Evans again proved that their Texan counterparts in terror and blood-letting were merciful by comparison.

They were to prolong the terror and suffering for at least another day. Their unquenchable lust had still not been satisfied. Evans drove back to Barna to get supplies and dispose of some of the victim's clothes. He returned later to Ballinahinch where Shaw had obviously continued the abuse and torture. Evans took over while Shaw went to Roundstone for a drink. When he returned the decision was made to kill the victim.

Shaw first put a cushion over her head and then, manually, strangled the life out of the girl who would be later identified as Mary Duffy, a delicately built twenty-four-year-old shop assistant. Her agony was now over. The pair took off all her clothes, put her body into the back of the car and again went in search of water to hide the evidence of their foul deed. They found it nearby at Lough Inagh.

They went through the same routine as before, getting a boat as well as weights to ensure that the body would reach and stay on the lake bed. The body was placed in the middle of the boat and an anchor, brick and sledgehammer were tied around Mary Duffy's waist. In the pitch black they rowed out into the dark waters of the lake and chose a spot.

As they attempted to lift the body overboard the weights nearly capsized the boat. They took the operation more carefully and the pathetic bundle slipped under the surface of the lake and, dragged by the weight, moved slowly but surely towards the lake bed.

As they rowed blind in the darkness, Shaw and Evans could have got lost in the vast expanse of the lake but while they missed the starting point by some distance the two safely made the shoreline on the same side. They collected the victim's clothes, returned to the car and drove back to Ballynahinch, where they made a bonfire of some of their own and Mary's clothes. They then decided to go back to the lake and return the boat from where they had stolen it. It really did not make a lot of difference but it demonstrated just how cold and calculating they were.

Mary was not reported missing until the evening of September

24 giving the murderers a head start before any missing persons operation got seriously underway. Such an operation is by its nature slow and labour-intensive, involving house-to-house inquiries and questionnaires. But even though time was on Shaw and Evans's side, the inevitable connection between the disappearance of Mary and Elizabeth was made. This, matched with the details including the registration number of the car supplied by the Maam shopkeeper, gave the investigation team a very strong lead.

Shaw and Evans were oblivious to these developments, locked as they were in their own depraved fantasies. They were on the look-out for their next victim. But at last their luck was beginning to run out. Driving to Galway they picked up another woman who, sensing the danger, asked to stop at a pub to go to the toilet. She escaped out the back.

The killers continued their journey. They reached Galway and on the night of September 26 parked the car on the prom in Salthill, a popular holiday spot and a place where unsuspecting women might take a walk. But such was the depth of their compulsion that they did not realise that they might as well have been parked on a main road. While they were having a drink in a nearby hotel, two gardaí on patrol noted the car and the registration number and, not wanting to risk using the radio, one ran to the nearby Garda station for reinforcements. Just then Shaw and Evans appeared and got into the car. The patrol car blocked the way and an officer took Evans from the car just as reinforcements arrived. Both men were arrested and brought to Eglington Street Garda Station in Galway. It was the end of the road for Ireland's first serial killers.

Two days later the body of Elizabeth Plunkett was washed ashore near Duncormack on the south Wexford coast. But it would take an exhaustive search to find Mary Duffy's remains despite an outing to Lough Inagh under Garda escort when the killers pointed to the spot where her body was dumped. Garda, army and civilian divers took part in the operation in teams of seven to cover the lake bottom.

The thirty divers were hampered by the fact that the bed of the lake was covered by a layer of silt and mud, which threw up an impenetrable cloud. A further complication was the depth and temperature of the water, which limited the divers to no more than one hour in the lake. The body of Mary Duffy was eventually discovered on the afternoon of October 10, 1976 and had been very well preserved in the freezing temperatures.

He has looked into the eyes of psychopaths, serial killers, murderers, rapists, career criminals and common thieves. He has experienced enough of evil to have lost his reason or sunk inexorably into the black pit of cynicism. But, miraculously, retired Detective Inspector Gerry O'Carroll speaks of his twenty-five years of murder investigation with equanimity and an understanding born of instinct and natural intelligence.

Apart from what he would term the routine murders, if one can call any killing routine but covering incidents in which it occurs such as robbery, fights and domestic conflict, O'Carroll encountered the more heinous category of serial killing. His instinct, grasp of psychology and unusual interrogating methods proved extremely successful.

At the time of Shaw and Evans's arrest in Galway Gerry O'Carroll was one of the famous detective flying squad team which included John Courtney, Mick Canavan, Thomas Ibar Dunne and Hubert Reynolds. When the Galway team were not making any progress with the prisoners, the Dublin-based Murder Squad were called on and travelled west. O'Carroll recalls:

> I couldn't find any accommodation, so I decided to sleep in the station. After going for a long walk I returned quite late. I had a cup of tea and a sandwich and just hung about. As the night wore on I thought to myself, maybe I will have a conversation with John Shaw, on the basis that you never know what might come out of it. I got him taken out of his cell and brought to a billiard room on the second floor.
>
> I just chatted easily with him and asked about his childhood in Wigan. He was Catholic and we talked about First Communion and Confirmation. He began to loosen up. I said to him that I wondered what happened from the time one was a young innocent boy to a man who was capable of murder and why that should be. It was a shock that a human being could murder a young, beautiful girl in the presence of another man.

Shaw put his head in his hands and sighed and the detective knew that he was vulnerable. He suggested that they pray together.

> I began to recite the Hail Mary and suddenly he gripped me by the arm. An expression of fear crossed his face and he cried out that he could see the devil. I

had been wondering about Mary Duffy who was missing and we didn't know if she was alive. He let out another roar about the devil. Then an expression of abject terror crossed his face – 'I see Mary Duffy, there, there,' he cried.

I knew that moment that she was dead and we had Ireland's first serial killers. He then blurted out the whole horrific story of how he and Evans had performed unspeakable acts on the victims before the killings. Ironically he said he was glad that they had been caught because they had planned to murder one woman every week. At 3.30 a.m. I brought in Detective Sergeant Tom Connolly and we took a full statement from Shaw which he signed. We did the same with Evans.

In February 1978 John Shaw and, ten months later in December, Geoffrey Evans were found guilty of the murders of Elizabeth Plunkett and Mary Duffy and are still serving their sentences in prison. They are the longest-serving murderers in the history of the State and it is Gerry's opinion that they, like the Moors murderers, should never be let out again.

His second encounter with a multiple killer was the 1983 case of the murder of three Irish soldiers on UN peace-keeping duty in the Lebanon. Corporal Morrow and Privates Byrne and Murphy were serving with the 52nd battalion, Cathal Brugha Barracks, and at their post near Tbnin when they lost their lives in an apparent gun attack. A fourth member, Private Michael McAleavy, survived and claimed that the attack was carried out by PLO guerrillas. But ballistic evidence proved that bullets which caused the deaths of his colleagues came from his gun. After months of interrogation by UN and Irish Army personnel, McAleavy stuck to his story.

> The Irish Army authorities requested the Garda to provide an interrogation team and myself, the late Chief Superintendent Dan Murphy, a great policeman and mentor, DI Pat Culhane and Detective Sergeant Tom Connolly were flown out to Beirut. It was just in the aftermath of the Israeli invasion and the Lebanon was in a frightening state, bearing all the scars of war and a very dangerous place to be.

> There was a very eerie atmosphere and a chilly emptiness as we passed through Beirut and drove under armed escort on the long road to Nakura. There we were briefed and brought to Camp Shamrock, the Irish battalion area. The enclosure where McAleavy was being held was called Gallows Green. The building was pockmarked with shells and blankets were draped over the holes in the roof.

> The accused was sitting in a chair under armed guard when we arrived and we requested the soldiers to leave. The ballistic evidence removed any doubt about his guilt but we needed to get a statement, and the truth, not the story that he had made up which was patently untrue. I sat in a chair opposite him. Suddenly he leapt to the floor and set down on all fours. 'I am a werewolf,' he shouted, 'and when the

moon is full I howl.' He then began to howl like a wolf. I told him quietly but firmly that we had not flown thousands of miles and travelled through a dangerous war zone to listen to a man giving an imitation of a werewolf.

If he was trying to convince us that he was mad, he wasn't doing a very good job of it, so I asked him to get off the floor. He got back on the seat and within a matter of minutes he admitted the killings. He said that the other soldiers were laughing at him. Earlier, as part of that four-man team, McAleavy had had a row with an Israeli officer who had refused to show his identification at a checkpoint. McAleavy had pointed his rifle at the officer.

He was then admonished by Corporal Morrow who allowed the Israeli officer through. The corporal told McAleavy that he was going to report the incident on the basis that his action could have jeopardised their safety. Corporal Morrow then returned to his post. McAleavy claimed he heard the group laughing and he approached them, opened up the breach of the rifle and gunned them down, moved in and fired again.

The killer was later discovered to have anti-semitic prejudices and an obsession with Hitler and the Third Reich. He was found guilty of the murders at a military court and jailed. He is now free.

One of the things that disturbs me is the absence of

any mandatory sentence for murder. We all know that life imprisonment with 99% of cases means anything but life. Nobody even serves the full length of the sentence handed down. There have been mandatory sentences brought in for a number of crimes including drugs but the most heinous crime, that of deliberately taking a life, is a hit and miss process.

The proliferation of murder since I began in the force is staggering. Once it merited front-page headlines. Nowadays, unless there is high profile or highly unusual circumstances, a paragraph will suffice. Serial killing has also appeared on the map in a much more common way. Shaw and Evans were the exception in the seventies. It is inconceivable that the disappearance of a number of young women such as Deirdre Jacob, Fiona Pender and Annie Mc Carrick in one small area of the country is coincidental.

The connecting factor is that they have disappeared without trace and any detective will tell you that this is a difficult thing to achieve and that in most cases, even if a body is buried in the remotest of parts, it usually turns up. And not only have the bodies not turned up but there have been no clues and not one iota of evidence. Studies of serial killers prove that they are very clever people and are often only caught by chance or by their desire to stop murdering when they deliberately leave clues.

5
SPINNING OUT OF CONTROL

The late Vinnie Connell was a control freak whose attitude towards women was intensely predatory. He pillaged their emotions, violated them physically and sexually and used his charisma to use and abuse them and put them down at every opportunity. He exploited his position to seduce, then threaten and dominate women, instilling a sense of fear and dread that made some of them find it difficult or even impossible to escape his pervasive influence.

In the mid-eighties he became a suspect for the murder of Patricia Furlong at the Fraughan Festival, an annual event held in Glencullen near the Dublin mountains in south County Dublin. Patricia, a pretty twenty-one-year-old shop assistant, had gone to the festival on the evening of July 23, 1982. Sometime before 1.00 a.m. she was seen in the vicinity of the main marquee talking to a tall man dressed in white. The following morning her half-naked body was found in a nearby field. She had been strangled with a ligature fashioned out of her upper garments.

Typical of a random killing, it proved hugely difficult to solve even though it had taken place only a short distance from where a large number of people had gathered. Witness statements had also to be tempered by the fact that, by that time of the night, a lot of alcohol had been consumed. There was no apparent link between perpetrator and victim and there was no forensic evidence.

Connell, a well-known pirate radio station DJ, had a special reason to be present that night. One of the major sponsors was RTÉ Radio 2 and he knew that there would be important executives of the station at the function whom he might be able to impress. He dressed to stand out – all in white. He was tall and good-looking with a silver tongue, he was in a perfect situation to promote his talent. And he was a true believer in his destiny.

He had worked at a number of previous low-profile (in his estimation) jobs including as a prison warden. He desperately wanted to be recognised as somebody of importance and substance, and radio was the perfect medium to sell himself to the public. He wanted to hit the legitimate airwaves where he perceived that he would have real power.

Vinnie Connell was a smooth talker, a charmer and highly attractive to the opposite sex, whose demeanour gave no hint of what lay bubbling beneath the surface. He had, like many killers, a deeply imbedded hatred of women. An absent father figure in the early stages of childhood development is often thought to provide an explanation for this trait and is apposite in this instance.

Brought up in middle-class respectability in Terenure, south County Dublin, Vinnie's father died when he was a young boy and he was reared by his doting mother and a maiden aunt. The boy was part of an all-female household and one that spoilt him, failing to impose any domestic discipline. It proved to be a ruinous method of nurture because this boy got used to getting his own way and behaved abominably without any hint of retribution. It was untrammelled behaviour that he would carry into adulthood with dire consequences.

Connell's propensity for violence towards women was not

something that manifested in adulthood. As an unruly and obnoxious teenager he beat up his mother and aunt so badly that they had to be hospitalised. They did not report him to the police and so unwittingly paved the way for years of torture, beatings and death threats to the other women in his life.

In the unbalanced domestic environment, Vinnie Connell was used to getting his own way all of the time and behaving how he liked without constraint. Children such as him with other problems of imbalance tend to react to ordinary disappointment with a far more intense sense of misery and defeat than better adjusted children.

Such children, going unpunished, develop an extreme kind of self-indulgence that appears to be insanity but in fact is a very cold and conscious form of evil. The unwillingness of his guardians to teach a lesson to the violent brat would ensure that Vinnie, as he grew up, got used to the idea of getting away with murder. In his own mind he was a person who was beyond punishment. If there was anyone to deal that out, it would be him.

Ironically he was never short of the company of vivacious, attractive and intelligent women, who were taken in by a seemingly confident, smart and ambitious character. But it would not take much time for the disguise of charm to be replaced by the mask of hatred. A colleague in the pirate station Sunshine Radio reeled back in shock one day when he made an enquiry about Connell's latest in a long line of love companions.

'I hit the bitch with a hammer,' he replied. 'I only broke her shoulder. It's a pity that I didn't kill her.'

The boy had not left the man and the vicious teenager had now become a psychopath. Naturally, the terrified woman did not report this assault, giving Connell the licence to continue his evil ways.

On the night of the murder of Patricia Furlong, Connell was in the company of his then girlfriend Mary Creedon. At one stage he told her that he had to leave the beer tent to meet a friend. It was a detail that Creedon omitted to tell investigators at the time. He was in fact meeting Patricia Furlong whom neither Creedon nor the gardaí knew had a link with the killer. They knew each other from the Top Hat ballroom in Dun Laoghaire where he choreographed a roller disco team which Furlong had ambitions to join.

They went to a nearby field and chatted for a while. The rakish Connell probably made a sexual advance and then flew into one of his violent rages when rejected. He knocked Patricia to the ground, pulled off her clothes from the waist up and, incensed by her rejection, used her tee-shirt as a garrote to strangle her. This was what most likely gave him the greater sexual thrill – extreme violence with murderous intent.

Roughly forty-five minutes later he returned to the tent and left with his girlfriend around 1.30 a.m. On the way home Mary Creedon noticed that he was sullen and in bad humour. He asked her to go away with him to Scotland the next day but she refused as it had come up out of the blue with no explanation.

The following evening, when he was routinely questioned by investigators, Connell flew into a rage and left the Garda station, dragging Mary away with him. While the team may have thought this behaviour odd, Connell had a cast-iron alibi provided by his girlfriend who said that he had been with her in the tent all the time. His rage was probably prompted by his absolute disdain for authority and the outrageousness of having to account for himself on any level, as opposed to any sense of fear or guilt.

Three weeks later detectives visited Connell at his home. At first he seemed relaxed and friendly but he turned, as one detective said, at the drop of a hat. When the detective had written down Connell's account of his movements and the people he met on the night of the murder and asked him to sign the statement, Connell flew into a rage and asked the detectives to leave, saying that he would report them to the commissioner for hassling him.

Connell did leave for Liverpool some days later and landed a job with Radio City where his talent and smooth-talking style landed him a top afternoon slot. But back at home Mary Creedon had been bothered by the fact that he had persuaded her to lie about the alibi. Although she was engaged to be married to him she told confidantes that she did not love him. After a discussion with close friends she determined to break off the relationship.

She travelled to Liverpool and when they met, Mary informed Connell of her intention to break off the engagement. One thing that men of his character abhor is rejection of any kind. It is not what they are used to, no matter how badly they behave. They have a total and irrational conviction that they are right about everything and of the stupidity and foolishness of anyone who opposes them. It is their prerogative to determine an outcome in business or their personal life. A woman has no right to make such decisions.

Connell flew into one of his characteristic rages, beat her and kept her prisoner in his flat for the next three weeks. When he went to work he left her handcuffed to the bed. During this period he continually abused her both physically and sexually. He had Mary exactly where he wanted her and all women – as his slave. Luckily Mary managed to escape. She made contact with her family in Dublin who came to Liverpool and took her home.

From then on Mary lived in fear and terror of Connell. One time when he persuaded her to meet him, he tried to strangle her and subsequently threatened to burn down her family home. Again he was not reported and his reign of abuse and terrorising of women continued unabated.

In 1983 Connell was sacked by Radio City and he took a case for unfair dismissal against the management. The station's then chief reporter Kieran Devaney was visiting Dublin and was asked by his boss to make enquiries into the background of the sacked DJ. He discovered first of all that Connell had given the station false references. He was soon made aware of Connell's connection to the Furlong murder and he made an appointment to meet Mary Creedon. She told him about the false alibi she had given because Connell had threatened her. She subsequently made a statement to that effect to the Garda investigating team.

By then Connell had moved on, this time to South Africa. While in Liverpool he had met a South African girl, Belinda Crane, who persuaded her wealthy parents to pay for his fare to Johannesburg. Within weeks his charm had worked and he talked himself into a job at Radio 5, a national broadcasting music station. He soon became a household name and took over the anchor job on a hugely popular Sunday morning chat show.

Through his show he raised money for charity, most notably in the case of two children in need of liver transplants. With supreme irony, in the light of a later revelation, Connell won an award from the South African Society for the Prevention of Cruelty to Animals for the success of his show in finding homes for stray dogs and cats. He also, with considerable success, took on the role of a lay preacher.

His compulsion was not diminished by either change of circumstance – he was now the embodiment of substance and importance he longed to be – or location in the higher echelons of South African society. Like the Ripper, Connell became a master of disguise but his psychopathic tendencies were never far from the surface.

He married a single parent Felicity Louw in Port Elizabeth in 1987. It was a marriage made in hell. He routinely beat his wife and her teenage daughter Sally. While he smiled in public and played the role of the popular personality, he portrayed all the attributes of Jekyll and Hyde and was a devil at home. He told Felicity that his charity work had one purpose – to further his radio career. He would laugh at her when she accused him of having a dual personality. Her daughter described him as a brutal man with an uncontrollable temper. After one savage attack on his wife who believed she was going to be killed, he was forced to flee South Africa.

He ended up in Namibia where he landed another radio job. It was a big climb down from his previously elevated position and his self-esteem took a dive. He took to the drink, was suspended from the station and sunk into a deep depression. A feature of his talent, however, was an ability to reinvent himself. He was simply too arrogant to accept humiliation which he would always, as is typical of his kind, blame on anyone but himself.

In 1989 he heard of the proposed issuing of independent radio licences in Ireland and decided to return. He landed a job with Capital Radio but was let go as part of a cost-cutting exercise. In the meantime investigators of the Furlong murder had reopened the case. Connell was arrested in The Fleet bar in Dublin city centre by then Detective Sergeant Gerry O'Carroll under Section 30 of the Offences against the State Act for alleged offences unrelated to the murder: assault, attempted strangling and arson. Two days later, after signing a confession, he was charged with the murder of Patricia Furlong.

During the subsequent investigation a number of his former girlfriends and their families were interviewed and a trail of horrendous abuse and violence was revealed. This included assault and arson committed against Mary Creedon, Gillian Kane, Agnes Long and Barbara Rooney. On two occasions he had set fire to the house of one of his girlfriends while she and her parents were inside. He had attempted to strangle Mary Creedon, Agnes Long and Barbara Rooney and he had assaulted all three.

In 1980, while in Gillian Kane's house waiting for her to get ready for an evening out, he began to strangle the family dog, at the same time screaming that his girlfriend loved the dog more than him. Gillian's mother intervened and took the dog away from him. Some weeks later the dog disappeared and the family were convinced that Connell had abducted and killed the animal. The killing of animals in advance of humans is a well-known trait of psychopaths.

In December 1991 after forty-two days, one of the longest criminal trials at the time in the history of the State, Connell was found guilty of the murder of Patricia Furlong and sentenced to life imprisonment. His South African ex-wife Felicity Louw had been approached to give evidence in the trial but refused because she was still terrified of him and wanted to forget she ever knew him.

Four and a half years later the verdict was overturned by the Court of Criminal Appeal on a number of technicalities relating to his detention and questioning while in custody in Tallaght Garda Station. It was a huge blow to the family of the victim and the investigators, not alleviated by the fact that he was found guilty of the arson and assault charges for which he received a suspended sentence of twelve years. No one involved in the case or indeed the family had any doubt that Connell was responsible for the murder.

During a bail application in the Four Courts on a second series of charges in May 1995 Connell suffered a heart attack. It was the beginning of serious health problems which led to his death alone in a flat in Portsmouth, England three years later. He was forty-eight years of age but could have been mistaken for a man well into his sixties.

What is not at issue for investigators such as Gerry O'Carroll, who had direct dealings with him, and a forensic psychiatrist is that Vinnie Connell possessed all the characteristics of a serial killer, most obviously the Jekyll and Hyde persona. He could change from a charming, intelligent and charismatic figure into a man capable of monstrous violence exclusively aimed at women. According to Gerry O'Carroll,

> He was the most complex mix of a human being that I ever came across. He was the most evil man I ever met. He had a magnetic personality with the most

incredible capacity to reinvent himself. He worked as a prison officer, disc jockey, policeman in Liverpool, a star radio personality and lay preacher in South Africa and, bubbling always to the surface, was a devious liar and a cruel, vicious brute who had murdered one woman and attempted to murder four people, and wreaked havoc in the lives of those he encountered, particularly women.

According to O'Carroll, Vinnie Connell had all the hallmarks of, and was one step away from becoming, a serial killer. His wife in South Africa told the detective that he was the most evil man she had ever met and she feared for her life and that of her two children. She had no idea he was wanted for murder until her parents who were touring Ireland heard that a warrant had been issued for his arrest.

He had attempted to kill Felicity and after she divorced him he attacked another woman, Denise Raine, with a hammer and paralysed her on one side. In Ireland he firebombed the home of his then girlfriend Gillian Kane who barely escaped with her ailing parents.

Gerry O'Carroll has no doubt that this evil genius could have been responsible for the deaths of at least half a dozen women.

6
THE GRANGEGORMAN MURDERS

Sometime after midnight on March 7, 1997 a man entered a house attached to St Brendan's psychiatric hospital in Grangegorman, Dublin and committed a crime of savagery in some aspects unequalled in the canon of vicious murder in Ireland. There was no apparent motive and absolutely no connection between the victims and the killer. The horror at the scene, the implications of what had happened and the fact that the man responsible was walking the streets of Dublin shocked the most experienced and hardened of gardaí investigators.

Sylvia Shields (58) and Mary Callinan (61) were low-dependence psychiatric patients attached to the well-known mental hospital and lived in accommodation just outside the main entrance to the hospital complex. There was a third occupant of the house who for some reason the killer left alone. She heard nothing that night because she had fallen asleep with the headphones of her Walkman in place.

This patient, Ann Mernagh, last saw both women at about 7.45 p.m. on March 6 before she went out to bingo. She later saw Sylvia Shields in her bedroom at 11.40 p.m. when she asked her to give her a wake-up call in the morning. She went to bed and put on her headphones. She fell asleep and did not wake up until 6 a.m.

When she went downstairs she found the contents of her handbag at the foot of the stairs and, on entering the kitchen, saw that all the kitchen drawers had been pulled out. She went upstairs and without looking properly saw Sylvia Shields lying across the bed with her feet hanging down. She remarked, 'You should be in the bed, not out of it.' But when she focused she was confronted with a horrific sight.

She saw that her friend's throat had been cut and in shock put her hand on the body which she found was stone cold. Later she would learn that blood was found on the carpet of her own room. The killer had actually entered it at some stage during the night but Ann Mernagh had heard nothing of the bloody slaughter. She alerted neighbours and the gardaí were called.

When the State Pathologist John Harbison arrived he began his on-the-scene preliminary postmortem examination. He counted over forty wounds on each of the bodies of the victims, some of which had been inflicted after death. Both women had died from shock and haemorrage. In Sylvia Shields case the bleeding had been caused by multiple stab wounds to the head, neck and chest. Mary Callinan's bleeding was caused by multiple sharp weapon injuries to the head, neck and chest. There was mutilation to the breast and genital areas of both women also.

This was a ritual, sadistic killing of the most disturbing nature carried out by a psychotic and dangerous killer whose method of killing rivalled that of Jack the Ripper for both cruelty and perversity. There was some consolation, if that is the word, for the relatives of Sylvia Shields in the fact that the throat wound inflicted earlier on would have rendered her unconscious, sparing her the torture of the succeeding frenetic stabbing and mutilation.

Mary Callinan's face had been literally hacked to pieces to such an extent that she was unrecognisable. In the ferocity of the attack several of her ribs had been fractured. The wounds and the mutilation around her pelvic area had been inflicted after death, a method also employed by Jack the Ripper.

Two knives were recovered at the scene. The blade of one large knife had been bent by 180 degrees, while the blade of the smaller knife had been broken. The bodies were viewed at 7.20 a.m. by Dr James Moloney who calculated that the women had been dead for between six and twelve hours.

The inquest into the deaths of Sylvia Shields and Mary Callinan have been adjourned twenty-one times in the Dublin Coroner's court due to continued criminal investigations into the double murder.

7
THE WRONG MAN

More than four months after the Grangegorman murders, on July 26, 1997, a homeless drug addict Dean Lyons was arrested at a hostel and brought to the Bridewell Garda Station for questioning. Interrogators claimed that his social welfare card was found in the vicinity of the crime scene. At the time he was strung out on heroin and the thing utmost in his mind was getting a fix because he had begun, in junkie parlance, to 'get sick' from withdrawal symptoms.

Heroin addicts are known to be compulsive liars and to live in a fantasy world where the reality of ordinary-day life has no meaning. The only meaning is to get the next hit and the next one, just to feel normal. Any statement that Lyons would give would not only lack any credibility, but would be severely tested by a defence team in court on the basis that he was in no fit state to make admissions that were not heavily influenced by his needs at the time.

In addition Lyons, like all addicts, was a lightweight physical wreck with just about enough strength to find a vein. It must have been abundantly obvious that he had not the physique to carry out the murders. Nonetheless the interrogation continued and, in a later statement taken in August 2000 in Manchester about the arrest and questioning, Lyons recalled his increasing sense of panic and desperation as the withdrawal symptoms took a grip of his craving body.

The guards kept questioning me about the murders

and a while later I confessed. Back at that time in 1997 I was a very heavy heroin user; I took it daily by syringe. I was always feeling very sick and I had to get heroin every day. I remember the day I was arrested in July 1997 I was very sick and needed heroin. Before I was arrested I gave £60 to a friend of mine to get me a gram of heroin and I told him that I would meet him at the hostel at 12 midday. This was before I knew I was going to be arrested. While I was at the Bridewell Garda Station, I was so sick all I wanted to do was get out of the station to meet him.

When I say I was feeling sick, I mean I had pains and aches and cramps in my stomach and I couldn't deal with anything. All I wanted to do was get out of the station. I remember telling the guards that I was sick and wanted a doctor. In fairness, they sent for a doctor and when he came I told him I was coming down off heroin. The doctor left methadone for me. Much later in the evening I got the methadone but I was feeling sick all day.

When I started to admit to the murders, I thought I was going to get out of the station. I knew in my mind that I did not commit the murders but I thought if I admitted to them I would get out to get my heroin. After admitting the murder to the guards, I remember I had a visit from my father and I told him that I had committed the murders. I felt that after admitting the murder to the guards I couldn't tell my father that I didn't do them. I did not realise how much trouble I was in. When you are on heroin, you are all messed up and you cannot think straight.

I remember my first interview with the guards was on video and then I had a break and was put back in the cell. When I was being taken out of the cell to go back for the interview, one of the guards said to me, 'You look very tense on video, would you like to come off the video as you might be more relaxed?' I said, yes I would come off the video, and I said on tape I would come off the video. The interview was not then on video and I admitted the murders.

For those familiar with the behaviour of heroin addicts there are some strange inconsistencies about the statement. Addicts are notorious liars, rarely admit to any wrongdoing and blame everybody and anybody rather than themselves. It is entirely understandable that Lyons would want to get out of the station to score his fix but as a streetwise junkie he would know that the last way of achieving that objective would be by admitting guilt. That would result in the opposite – he would be kept in custody.

He blames this course on the confusion of addiction but there is clearly something more to his admission than simply throwing up his hands and saying, yeah, I did it, and then adding that he did not know how much trouble he was in. Despite his condition it could not have been clearer. The details of the murders would have had to have been discussed at length before any admission. It is inconceivable that Lyons, unless he had been led in the interrogation, could have possibly known anything about the scene of the crime or the injuries to the victims.

It should have been clear to his interrogators that the pathetic addict in front of them was mentally and physically incapable of a crime of this magnitude which was in the canon of the Whitechapel and Manson murders. Not, on any level, did Dean Lyons fit the bill. In addition to his heroin habit, he had learning difficulties, a morbid fear of authority and, like all junkies, was a fantasist. Nothing in his personality, background or behaviour suggested that he could inflict such a ghastly end on two mild and inoffensive mental patients.

Wider experience of such killings show that the suspects will make emphatic denials of any knowledge or involvement in the crimes and even if guilty will never give in until presented with undeniable evidence of their participation. This was not the case with Dean Lyons – he gave in far too easily to be a credible perpetrator.

And yet he was charged with the murder of Mary Callinan. One forensic expert was so appalled by the ineptitude of holding Lyons responsible for the murders that he told the investigation team, in no uncertain terms, that they had the wrong man and that the real killer was still on the loose, with the strong possibility that he would strike again. It was not simply the fact that they were holding a man incapable of committing such a crime but in the meantime other innocent people could become victims of a man described as a highly dangerous sexual psychopath. The expert's advice was ignored but he would be proved to be absolutely correct in his assessment.

Less than a month after Dean Lyons was arrested, Mark Nash, on the run after the murder of a man and a woman and the attempted murder of another woman, was arrested in Galway. While being questioned he admitted to the Grangegorman murders, revealing detail that only the killer would have known. He later retracted that confession. He is now serving life imprisonment for the double murder of Carl and Catherine Doyle who were stabbed to death in a frenzied attack in August 1997, just months after the Grangegorman killings.

Even in the immediate aftermath of Nash's admission, Dean Lyons was languishing in custody, despite the protests of the experts. He continued to be the official prime suspect while an internal Garda inquiry was held into his arrest and detention. The inquiry concluded what was glaringly obvious from the start – Dean Lyons was incapable of carrying out the Grangegorman murders. The sad and perhaps self-deluded young man was released without explanation and charges were dropped in February 1998.

Lyons died from a heroin overdose in Manchester shortly after giving the statement about his arrest. It was a sad chapter for his parents John and Sheila Lyons who to this day do not know the reasons why the Garda investigation team saw fit to persist so long with the myth that their late son had anything to do with the murders. The addicted young man was unable to wreak destruction on anybody but himself. The real killer was made of an entirely different mental character than the weak and vulnerable Dean Lyons.

8
PROFILE OF A KILLER

A leading forensic psychiatrist has provided a terrifying profile of the killer of the low-dependent patients Sylvia Shields and Mary Callinan. He also points out that, had the gardaí consulted a profiling expert at the time of the double murder the profile would have immediately ruled out Dean Lyons.

> The savage murders of these two women was a systematic butchering and ritual slaughter which a physically depleted drug addict of Lyon's frail stature would not have been capable of carrying out. The disorganised nature of an addict's life and scattered mentality is the opposite of this killer who, to judge from the huge amount of wounds sustained by the victims, is a physically robust man in his late twenties or early thirties.

> He is psychotic, deeply disturbed and probably suffering from extreme paranoia. This type of killer has fantasised about the act in advance and possibly staked out the location of the crime. A heroin addict would simply be intent, in such a situation, on stealing money to feed his habit. If inclined to violence, it would not be carried out in such a systematic fashion and the addict would not have the physical strength to sustain an attack that required considerable strength.

The killer is essentially a loner with poorly developed communication and social skills and if employed would not last long in a job or sustain a personal relationship. His poor grasp of reality outside his fantasies indicate that he was not employed or personally attached in any meaningful way at the time of the murders. There is little doubt that he had fantasised about such violence in advance of the act.

The expert says that the murders were carried out by a male with deep psychotic tendencies that had developed since childhood. He may have been raised by a lone parent, his mother, and lacked the presence of a father figure. This is a common factor in sexual psychopaths and serial killers who harbour anger and hatred for women because of some perceived wrong done to them by a dominant mother figure.

He has had a dysfunctional childhood and comes from a deprived background and, almost certainly, a broken home. Alone with his mother, he may have been exposed to a number of other males, none of whom filled the vacancy left by his father or developed any relationship with him. This would push him, as a child, to rely far more on a fantasy world to achieve some escape from the harshness of his family environment. Since nobody in his direct surroundings shows him any compassion, he develops a complete lack of compassion for others. This becomes more and more entrenched in his personality as he grows older.

Such a home life provides the learning school for his anger, resentment and ultimately violence. This background plays a crucial role in the development of serial killers and studies have provided consistent evidence of high instability in home life which include prominently hostile or poor relationships with the father and exposure to violence and sexual abuse.

Rightly or wrongly he blames his mother for his predicament, considers her immoral or worthless because she has had a number of male partners and has not paid enough attention to him. He blames her for the failures or disappointments in his life and will grow up full of bitterness and resentment which is transferred to females.

At the time of the murders, he is in his mid-twenties or early thirties when such resentments and paranoia peak. Previously he has satisfied his sadistic urges though fantasy and pornography.

According to the forensic psychiatrist, postmortem details including mutilation of the breasts and vagina and wounds in the pelvic area inflicted after death puts this killer into a very rare and dangerous category of sexual psychopath with obvious serial killing tendencies.

> This man is a very rare, disturbed, dangerous and perverted killer who may have killed before and after the Grangegorman murders. Traditionally this type, after murdering the victim, slashes, maims and cuts the body in the regions in and about the genitalia, rectum, breast and neck and around the throat and buttocks. These areas have some sexual significance for him and provide a sexual stimulus.

Such killers, if apprehended, he says, should never be freed, so great is the danger they pose to society and women in particular. Such systematic butchery is carried out by a sadistic, retarded personality who has no inhibition in the matter of violence, wants to instil terror in his victims and has no mercy and no remorse for his actions.

> He treats his victims as objects for his own pleasure, and the fact that he targeted two elderly women provides a key to his motivation. Most such sexual psychopaths choose young attractive women usually between the ages of seventeen and twenty-five. This is the predominant age group of the women who have been adbucted and disappeared in Ireland over the past decade. The choice of elderly victims is not unknown but is enough to identify the background of the killer.

> This unusual choice is a clear indication that the killer perceives that his mother rejected him and he has chosen to kill elderly women as an act of revenge against his mother for this rejection. The ferocity of this attack is a barometer of his hatred for his mother, as is the mutilation of the corpses and destruction of the genitalia. In his crazed fantasy the victims are wiped out and replaced by the image of his mother. Such killers often inflict such injuries that will render the victims unrecognisable as anyone other than the fantasy hate object. At the same time the victims are depersonalised, rendered meaningless as a result.

The killer, according to the psychiatrist, is a very sick man, inclined to go on a rampage of violence with no thought for the victims. Neither does he consider the risk of his being apprehended. His mind is in a constant state of self-delusion. As well as the Jekyll and Hyde personality, he is a Walter Mitty, dropping well-known or famous names as acquaintances. He will also constantly lie about his occupation or lack of it.

It is likely that he has boasted of his violent activities and told people that he has killed or maimed but was not believed because of his Walter Mitty character and the obvious lies and contradictions in his stories.

There are many frightening aspects to the character of this killer, not least the parallel to the physical mutilation carried out by Jack the Ripper. There is no suggestion that this is a copycat method or that he has any knowledge of the Whitechapel murders. But what is truly worrying is the mindset of a man who could carry out such acts of unadulterated savagery and the likelihood that he can and will, given the opportunity, repeat such killings. And all experts agree that he will.

It is worth then, given the danger to the public posed by this man, to draw a historical parallel with a serial killer with a similar mentality and childhood syndrome.

On September 9, 1973 a thirteen-year-old runaway, Jeri Billings, was hitchhiking in northeast Minneapolis. A truck pulled up driven by a large, bald man with a receding chin. After he had driven for a short distance, he unzipped his trousers and made her perform fellatio. Then driving on he ordered her to remove her jeans and panties. He forced a hammer into her vagina and then made her fellate him again. He then hit her on the head with the hammer.

Stopping the truck, he dragged her into a field and attempted to sodomise her but failed. He then allowed her to dress, drove her to a nearby town and told her to tell no one what had happened. After two months she reported the incident to the police. But the perpetrator had long gone.

In January 1974 a man with the same description stopped to help three women whose car had broken down. One, an attractive twenty-eight-year-old called Eileen Hunley, subsequently dated the man but, put off by his drinking and quick-fire temper, told him that she did not want to see him anymore. On August 10 of the same year, she disappeared.

A month later on September 8 two teenage girls, June Lynch and Lisa King, were hitchhiking in Minneapolis when a large middle-aged man stopped to offer them a lift. He later turned off the road into a wooded area and asked June Lynch to go with him. Lisa heard her friend scream and went to see what had happened. June was lying on the ground, bleeding from the head and the man had fled. In hospital it was established that the victim had been hit on the head seven times with a blunt instrument. She survived.

On September 14 the big man, driving a green Chevrolet, offered a lift home to a nineteen-year-old girl, Gwen Burton, whose car had broken down. When they were outside the town he grabbed her and forced her to fellate him. Then he ripped off her clothes and underwear and battered her. She recovered to find herself lying on a blanket in a field. The man forced her to carry out a perverse sex act and then inserted a hammer handle into her vagina. He then attacked her with the hammer.

The victim woke up and dragged herself to a roadway where she got help and was rushed to hospital. Gwen recovered but was permanently disabled.

On September 18, 1974 the body of a woman was found north of Minneapolis. She had been killed with a blunt instrument and her vagina had been lacerated by an object, probably a hammer handle. She was identified as Eileen Hunley. Two days later an eighteen-year-old girl, Kathy Schultz, disappeared from Minneapolis. The following day her body was found forty miles away by two hunters. She had been killed with blows from a hammer.

By now investigators had a good description of the man who had attacked the women who had survived and was suspected, by his modus operandi, of being involved in the unsolved murders. They were looking for a middle-aged, big, bald man driving, at this stage, a green Chevrolet. On September 24 two policemen saw a man answering that description. When the patrol car approached him he drove away at speed but was eventually forced off the road by the police.

The driver identified himself as Harvey Carignan and, when four of his surviving victims picked him out at an identity parade, his career was at an end. On February 14, 1975 he was tried on charges relating to Gwen Burton. His defence entered an insanity plea and the accused told the jury that he had been prompted to his action by messages from God. The jurors chose to disbelieve this and found him guilty.

He was subsequently tried and found guilty of the attack on the schoolgirl Jeri Billings, the murder of Eileen Hunley and unexpectedly he pleaded guilty to the murder of Kathy Schultz. He was sentenced to sixty years. There were up to a dozen other murders that he was almost certain to have committed but there was no evidence to convict him.

After the Burton trial Carignan was sent to the state hospital for psychiatric examination. The result was another classic example of the mental make-up of a serial killer. He was the illegitimate child of a young doctor who chose not to accept the responsibility and left his son's upbringing to the seventeen-year-old mother. Carignan was an undersized, lonely child who wet the bed far beyond the usual age. His mother, who felt that he had interrupted her life, showed him little affection. 'She was pretty mean,' he told psychiatrists. His mother married when he was four and then had a second son. As the bed-wetting became worse he was sent to live with an aunt and uncle. They got fed up with him and sent him back to his mother. He was later sent to a reform school where he was incarcerated from the age of twelve until he was eighteen.

In order to escape from his unhappy environment he became an incessant daydreamer. He was, like many of the kind he was to become, highly intelligent, charming and given any other start in life might have been successful. But he was poisoned with anger and resentment against women whom he claimed had sexually assaulted him as a child. This explanation was not accepted and the hatred bred by the rejection of his mother was deemed a far more plausible reason for his savage ways.

His frustrated craving for affection turned into a craving for power over the women who denied it, and the sexual craving and potency was transformed into a physical rage and the desire to obliterate.

In her book on Carignan, *The Want-Ad Killer,* Anne Rule summed up the type of killer:

> There is, today, no known treatment that is effective in changing the structure of the antisocial personality. The defect is believed to originate in childhood, usually before the age of five, and once the child is so damaged, his complete lack of compassion for others only becomes more solidly entrenched as he grows to manhood.

It is an opinion with which the forensic psychiatrist who profiled the Grangegorman killer concurs.

> It is a well-established fact that the most formative and lasting development in a human's life is in the early years of childhood. That is where the seeds of the future are sown. The problems are compounded as the child grows into adolescence and manhood. For those who develop a psychotic state of mind, there is no cure and no turning back. The damage is irreparable. Nobody is safe if these people are on the streets because they have no concept of the value of human life and as little respect for their own lives as those of their victims.

The normal inhibitors that stop the majority of men from translating their worst fantasies into reality are not present. The sense of responsibility, fear of shame and punishment that prevent the majority from committing crime are not operational, and the guilt and remorse that most human beings feel after having done something wrong is absent.

Everyone has fantasies be it about sex, fame, personality, power or money. Most people know where the border with reality exists and how to leave the fantasy where it properly belongs. Fantasy is a very healthy part of growing up – watch any three- or four-year-old at play for an afternoon and see how a large part of the play is based on the imaginary. But the psychotic sex killer lives increasingly in the world of fantasy and has no inhibition about translating the most heinous and lurid imaginings into reality.

And a great part of that fantasy has to do with power, the sort of power that the killer of young, beautiful Raonaid Murray wielded over his victim, that John Crerar had over Phyllis Murphy, Shaw and Evans over Elizabeth Plunkett and Mary Duffy and the Grangegorman killer over Mary Callinan and Sylvia Shields. The irony is that power is exercised by men of weak character and low self-esteem – an expression of dominance by humans who would normally be placed in a low-dominance category.

Murder has always been with us but this type of killer has only emerged relatively late in the history of many countries – the second half of the twentieth century in Ireland. It coincided with a time of progress and achievement when material values took a greater role, elevating fame and fortune as the goal for many. The needs of everyone become greater under such circumstances and unfulfilled needs can have disastrous consequences.

Both people and animals in overcrowded, competitive and stressful conditions can behave violently, with those of low-dominance and self-esteem being particularly vicious. American psychologist Abraham Maslow observed that if a new monkey is added to a group of monkeys, the newcomer often gets beaten up, the attack frequently led by a previously non-dominant monkey. He noted that this monkey would often behave with extreme ferocity, as if making up for its former inferior status. This provided a parallel with the sadistic behaviour of killers with low self-esteem attempting to gain dominance over their victims.

The implications of these facts are very clear. There is only one place for a psychopathic killer – behind bars for life. But that is by no manner or means guaranteed under the Irish criminal law system which has again and again proved, with notable exceptions, that the interests of the victims, their families and the public are often secondary to the rights of the perpetrators.

9
THE MURDERS OF
CARL AND CATHERINE DOYLE

The dreadful thing about murder is the thought that the victim's life was moving inexorably towards that final moment and every step along their life path is sullied and tinged with the sadness of the end. The victim has passed on but the family left behind are themselves victims until relieved by their own deaths. The effects of murder are far more complex and long lasting than the act itself.

The Doyle family from Clonsilla were decent working-class people. Pat and Catherine had seven children, one of whom, Catherine, met her future husband, Carl, at school in Kilbarrack where they were both pupils and in their mid-teens. They were a devoted couple, very much in love and at twenty-one years of age Catherine became pregnant with their eldest son Jesse. They married in a civil ceremony at Molesworth Street registry office after the birth.

They had a second son two years later, Frank, named after another of the Jesse James gang and for a while the couple lived in overcrowded conditions with Catherine's parents who considered their son-in-law as one of the family. Eventually the couple were housed by the council in Darndale, a tough part of north County Dublin.

It was living there that gave Catherine the idea of moving to a rural part of Ireland believing the environment was not suitable for the upbringing of her children. Suburban local authority estates, just like the flat complexes of the inner city, were targets for drug dealers on top of the fact that the deprived children of those areas had a bleak future. They got in touch with Rural Resettlement, an organisation that specialises in helping urban dwellers find suitable housing in rural Ireland.

In 1993 they were offered a house in Castleteehan, Co Roscommon. The accommodation was rented but it was the first step in finding the safe environment they wanted for their children. They saved every penny to put towards a deposit for their own home. One day her mother got a phone call and her excited daughter told her that Carl and herself had found their dream home. Catherine senior and junior were very close and the daughter ended every conversation by telling her mother that she loved her.

It was a rambling two-storey farmhouse in the tiny Roscommon village of Carane, as far from Darndale as the moon is from the earth. It had three bedrooms, a solid-fuel cooker and was set in a rural haven of peace and tranquillity in which the only noise was that made by nature: the wind, the trees and the animals. The couple had two more children over the following two years.

Carl got a job as a butcher at the Avonmore meat factory in Ballyhaunis, Co Mayo while Catherine was a full-time mother. They were overjoyed with the safety and simplicity of their life and had little to worry about in regard to the wellbeing and welfare of their children. Jesse and Frank went to school in Enfield while Holly and Heather stayed at home with Catherine who was passionate about flowers and plants. They took to the country life with gusto. For

Catherine and Carl Doyle life was idyllic and they struck neighbours as warm, friendly and very happy.

They were happy enough to renew their wedding vows, this time in the Catholic church in Ballintubber. They had set the date, November 27, 1997, and the parish priest Fr Seamus Cox had visited them to make the arrangements. Catherine had planned to wear a purple Chinese dress while Carl was going for the traditional top hat and tails. They would never live to see the day.

Catherine's sister Sarah Jane and her boyfriend, Mark Nash, were coming to visit them.

On August 15, 1997 Nash left the advertising company where he had recently found work at about 5 p.m. He then picked up Sarah Jane and the two babies, one his from a previous relationship and one hers. They then went to Heuston Station where they boarded a train bound for Roscommon. En route Nash had two drinks and Sarah Jane a bottle of beer. The train arrived between 8.30 p.m. and 9 p.m. and the party were collected by Carl. On the way to the house they stopped in Ballintubber and bought a bottle of vodka, Southern Comfort and soft drinks. At some stage a €50 deal of cannabis was purchased.

By 9.30 p.m. they were sitting in the living room having a drink and smoking the dope. A flagon of cider had also been opened. There were a total of six children in the house. A number of polaroid photographs were taken during the course of the evening including one of Nash on the toilet. Around midnight Carl Doyle crashed out on the settee.

Nash had spent the previous forty-five minutes in the bathroom vomiting and with diarrhoea, presumably brought on by a combination of the drugs and drink. If that was the case, he would have flushed a lot of the intake out of his system. While in the toilet a compulsion to kill came over him.

The two Doyle sisters had gone upstairs to sort out the sleeping arrangements. They were in the bedroom with the door slightly ajar when Nash came up the stairs, carrying a metal tool used to open the fuel can on a Stanley range. According to Sarah Jane he had a crazed look in his eyes. He began to strike her with the weapon and when she pleaded with him asking him why he was doing it, he said, 'You have to die.' Catherine intervened and he attacked her. Then he pushed Sarah Jane down the stairs and hit her again and again until she lost consciousness. When she woke up she pretended to be dead.

Dragging herself out of the house, Sarah Jane managed to get down the road to the nearest neighbours who alerted the gardaí. They arrived at the house and gained entrance through the back door. They were faced with a scene of devastation and utter carnage. There was blood all over the place. Garda Sergeant John O'Gara found the body of Catherine Doyle in a large pool of blood in the kitchen. In the living room Carl Doyle was dead on the settee, also covered in blood. There was no sign of Mark Nash.

Catherine Doyle had been stabbed sixteen times with a kitchen knife and an attempt had been made to strangle her. Carl had been stabbed at least four times in the chest and there were knife fragments left in his body. Nash had literally gone crazy and created a bloodbath in the dream home of the Doyle family. Sarah Jane, seriously injured, was brought to hospital. She thankfully survived.

Had she died, her unborn child would have also perished, making the killer responsible for four deaths. A search was organised to find Nash and he was arrested in Galway the following day.

10
A REASON TO DISBELIEVE

Sometimes you do something for no reason.
Sometimes reality disappears.
– Letter from Mark Nash to Sarah Jane Doyle

Disingenuous could describe the sentiments expressed by this murderous man. Not a hint of guilt or remorse. A bald statement of fact from a man who viciously killed people nearest to the recipient of the letter and almost killed her. This statement confirms the mentality of a psychopathic killer, a reason to never, ever allow him to be free to repeat them. The prospect of any other scenario, fills the family of his victims with intense fear and horror.

Mark Nash is a remorseless, fantasy-driven individual who, by his own admission, has no grasp of reality. His obsessions spilled into a reality from which his victims' families will never recover. There is no apology in his words.

In another part of the letter he confirms why he should remain incarcerated for the rest of his life, a man who is beyond rehabilitation and redemption.

The thoughts in my head are all still violent. Why have I gone this way?

Nash's background is instructive in finding a reason why he killed Carl and Catherine Doyle and equally for the Grangegorman murders to which he confessed but later withdrew his admission. The search for a motive for the Doyle killings was explored to no particular effect in his trial in October 1998. Unfortunately then, and now, the evidence of forensic psychiatrists and profilers carry as little weight in court as it did in the Clutter murder trial. Luckily in this case the facts were not in dispute, but there are other cases that might be more contentious in which such evidence could have vital bearing.

Seemingly motiveless murders carry less weight than those inspired by greed, jealousy, robbery, hate and all those others listed under the category of 'intent'. The late Greg Murphy S.C. made a powerful defence for his client Nash centred round the question of why the accused committed the crime. In a strong summing up he described the murders as 'motiveless crime'. Murder is a crime of intent, he argued, which means that the killing must be accompanied by *mens rea* or malice aforethought. He said that Nash had no intention when he killed.

In the accused own words:

> I fucking flipped. I can't think. I have gone mad and I cannot help myself.

There was no reason, he claimed, for the killings. He lost control.

> That is the way it happened. It was a mixture of drink,
> being drunk, being sick, seeing a knife and paranoia.

That was Nash's answer to a question during the trial when he was asked why he had carried out the killings. It is the classical reaction of the psychotic killer to try to shift the blame on to some unexplained external force.

If it was classical, then Nash's background fitted: illegitimate child, absent father. His mother, Bernadette, from Ballina, Co Mayo, emigrated to Huddersfield, West Yorkshire in England in the early 1970s. Mark was conceived after a relationship with a Jamaican man whose identity he never discovered. He was born in Mayo in 1974 and a year later he and his mother returned to England and settled in a working-class area of Bradford.

He contended that his mother was a prostitute and was very strict with him, showing no affection or love towards him. When drunk he told his girlfriend Sarah Jane that his father had left before he was born and that his mother used to take it out on him, beating him with a vacuum cleaner and the stiletto heel of her shoe. He later told psychiatrist Dr Richard Blennerhassett that deep down he believed that he was a 'trick baby', the unwanted product of a sexual liaison between prostitute and client.

Deeply ashamed of his background, he presented his parents as being wealthy, his father alternately a Jamaican or an Italian businessman. The fact was that he never knew his father, and his mother, however tenuous her relationship with the Jamaican was, did her already disadvantaged child no favours by isolating him further. Psychiatrist Dr Blennerhassett summed it up in evidence thus: 'His mother did not love him. He did not love his mother.'

It was his account and not confirmed by the mother but if only half true then as a child he would have been exposed to a number of men who had no fatherly responsibility. He had no sense of place in a family and worse still no grasp of his own identity. He returned on occasions to Ballina but all contact ceased with his grandparents when he was seven. Whatever little identity or familial base he had vanished. A tough place for any child to come from. Displaced personally, he attended a local Catholic school, All Saints High. He was rebellious and at twelve years of age began to drink and smoke cannabis. Although considered bright, he left school in 1990 at sixteen years of age. He later left home when he was eighteen after a series of disagreements with his mother.

After working in a solicitor's office he moved to Leeds where he worked for the Maxwell Corporation selling advertising. At seventeen, again classical for his type, he picked up a conviction for sexual assault. The charge was reduced to ordinary assault but the first sign on his future was posted.

He was using ecstasy and began dealing and got immersed in the drug scene. Two years later he met a girl called Lucy Porter and began a relationship. They lived in Hareshill, a suburb two miles from the centre of Leeds, above a shop. Nash fancied himself as a hard man in the drugs scene and this fantasy was fed by a film with which he was obsessed: Quentin Tarantino's blood-letting debut *Reservoir Dogs* which was heavily influenced by Hong Kong director Ringo Lam's *City Of Fire* as well as by Stanley Kubrick's *The Killing*. To a young and confused man in search of identity it provided a dangerous panacea. Derek Malcolm's review for *The Guardian* provided a chilling warning, entirely apt for this particular devotee.

> No one should go to see *Reservoir Dogs* without prior
> thought. But what they will see is a riveting treatment

on the theme of betrayal set in an urban wasteland
that murders hope and makes redemption virtually
impossible.

It was probably the character played by Harvey Keitel on whom
Nash modelled himself at that juncture. Later and more
distinctively it would be John Travolta as Vincent Vega in *Pulp
Fiction*. This is not speculation, it was acknowledged during the
trial by a psychiatrist who had interviewed Nash. *Reservoir Dogs*
deserves the warning from *The Guardian* critic. What marked this
film out from other practitioners of screen violence is the super-
realistic production of great quantities of blood and victim
suffering.

The aftermath of the shooting of a man during a failed heist in
this film is a case in point. Is it possible that a man would live so
long, suffer so much and should we call in a vascular surgeon to
establish if the wounds could possibly produce so much blood? It is
intensely graphic and a far cry from the chocolate sauce that
Hitchcock used in the famous shower scene in *Psycho*. Which
cinematically provides a case in point. The old master produced one
of the most frightening scenes of violence in cinema history. But in
the shower scene, where the character played by Janet Leigh is
murdered while showering by the unseen Norman Bates, nothing is
shown. This is in marked contrast to modern screen violence where
no grisly detail is spared the audience.

To most of us, such appalling violence whether naturalised or
stylised is hard to stomach but to the viewer with psychotic
tendencies it could seem like a feast for his fantasies.

The anticipation of violence, the planning and rehearsal of violence is the mark of the serial killer and the screen version must have provided a powerful stimulant to Nash. This is not to say that Tarantino or his film had any direct responsibility for the subsequent actions of this particular viewer. The mindset was well entrenched long before the release of the film.

Nash was obsessed with Tarantino's cool, confident criminal character in *Pulp Fiction* and the lightning fast, hip dialogue. He was entranced, saw the film countless times, could reproduce whole scenes of dialogue and began to affect the mannerisms, dress and hairstyle of the main gangster. It was an immature and childlike reaction to what Nash forgot was celluloid life and just what the title suggested – a piece of pulp fiction.

Dr Blennerhassett noted that Nash had taken on this persona:

> He is a self-confident man with a cocky exterior . . .
> who presents himself as a tough guy. He sees himself
> as the cool John Travolta-like figure in the film *Pulp
> Fiction*.

But the self-image was a sham, as unreal as the celluloid story in which his hero strutted his stuff and, when it came to the dangerous depths of the drug-dealing world, the real man, even with the sharp suits and the ponytail, wasn't up to it. Like many killers of his kind, he was a coward and could only deal out violence to those weaker and more vulnerable than himself.

Nash's alter ego and his obsession with Tarantino's graphic depiction of violence had an ironic echo in France around the time of his trial. Two high-profile trials were taking place there. In each case a woman was the main perpetrator. One had taken part in a shooting spree in which four people died and the other had incited her boyfriend to kill a boy for whom she harboured a sexual attraction.

Both women were, just as Nash was, obsessed with a film, in their case Oliver Stone's *Natural Born Killers* about a young couple on a mass murder spree who become media favourites. Without lapsing into a moral debate on the impact of screen violence, there is little doubt that sick minds can be heavily and destructively influenced by what is presented on screen.

In the light of events stimulation is almost precisely the effect that Tarantino's work had on Mark Nash, who at the time was trying to live out his fantasy of himself as a hard man, a role he was ill-suited to play with his peers. While Vincent Vega blows his opponents way with a .45, Mark Nash, ponytailed like his hero, runs. Such is the difference between the fantasy inspired by film and real life.

After a confrontation with a drug dealer and an arrest for dealing in cannabis, Nash fled to Dublin in 1996 with Lucy Porter. Their daughter was born in November of that year.

His relationship with Lucy was stormy, with frequent rows which veered towards violence. It wasn't long until the vicious streak appeared from beneath the Vincent Vega veneer. During one row he caught her by the hair and banged her head repeatedly off the side of the sofa. He threatened her with a steam iron and during another row put his hands around her neck and began to strangle her. He threatened to kill her when he found out that she had told a friend from whom he had borrowed a video recorder that he had sold it. Later, during questioning, he denied laying a finger on her, conceding that he may have banged her head against the sofa. Unsubtle and compulsive lying is another characteristic of his kind.

Lucy had had enough and Nash moved out of the flat and ended up in a hostel. After splitting with Lucy he would have been, as the Ripper put it, 'down on' women and in particular his mother whom he blamed for all his misfortune. He was now seething with bitterness and resentment and his thoughts became infected with fantasies of violence.

He admitted that one night, while walking home from town, he was overcome with a compulsion to kill. This was in March 1997 when the Grangegorman murders took place. At the time he was living under an assumed name at the Regina Coeli hostel for the homeless just north of the city and his self-esteem must have been particularly low. People of his mentality are highly dangerous at such times because their bitterness and anger against the world and other people is at high tide.

Nash told police that he had been at a charity reception in the GPO in Dublin on the night of March 6, 1997. He had a row with his ex-girlfriend Lucy Porter, who had agreed to meet him, and while walking home to the hostel was overwhelmed by a compulsion to kill. He broke into the house at Orchard View just outside Grangegorman hospital. After his arrest for the Roscommon murders six months later, Nash gave gardaí a detailed description of the interior of the house and the circumstances of the killings including the fact that the surviving woman had fallen asleep with her headphones on and consequently never heard anything. There is no way that he could have known such detail had he not been at the scene of the crime.

There were also striking similarities in the modus operandi of the killer in the Roscommon and Grangegorman murders. In both cases the victims were stabbed and slashed with unusual ferocity and force. In both cases the killer employed weapons of opportunity, knives obtained at the scenes of the crimes. The woman who slept through the Grangegorman murders, Ann Mernagh, identified Nash from photographs as a man she had seen the evening before staring at the house. Nash also admitted the murders to Sarah Jane Doyle in a letter from prison.

However, Nash, despite his confession and knowledge of the scene of the crime, has never been charged with the murders. He later, in the presence of a solicitor, withdrew the confession and now cannot be further questioned without his consent.

At the time of his admission Dean Lyons had already confessed and was being held in custody which created a dilemma and internal problems for the gardaí. This was hugely unfortunate because the investigation into the murder had narrowed, as it turned out, on the wrong man, preventing any focus from pointing at Nash.

As it transpired Nash had boasted on a number of occasions to some of his drug-taking 'business acquaintances' about the Grangegorman murders. His accounts did not in any way diminish the horrific nature of the killings. They had the effect of restoring his self-esteem. He was back in *Pulp Fiction* mode. Instead of feeling inhibited or ashamed of recounting the crime, Nash brought it up again and again to re-emphasise his new sense of self-respect as if he had repaid the world for all the wrongs done to him. Nash was always boasting of his acquaintance with well-known or famous people and some of his group took his utterances with a grain of salt. But after a time it dawned on them that he might indeed be talking of his own experience instead of borrowing it from the world of fantasy.

After his relationship with Lucy Porter had fallen apart he began to hang out more in the club scene. He mixed with a set who were heavily into drugs, mainly cocaine and ecstasy. Despite his nomadic existence he played the role convincingly of someone who was going places and from time to time managed to get a job which, characteristically, did not last long. While in this twilight zone of Dublin life he also craved respect and respectability. Some of his acquaintances managed to hold down jobs and run a business despite being devotees of the club scene. That is after all what cocaine is for – work, no rest and play.

It was in the Vatican club in April 1997 that he met Sarah Jane Doyle, a vulnerable eighteen-year-old, whom he tried to impress by saying that he was there with a number of business acquaintances. At the same time he was drinking water because he had no money. But he seemed to her to be self-assured, charming and good-looking in the manner of his own hero. Nash, as she was to find out, was another Jekyll and Hyde character.

Both would say later the relationship was a happy one to begin with. 'Things were fine and Mark and I got on well at first,' Sarah Jane said. She left the family home, with her baby from a previous relationship, and moved with him to the flat in Prussia Street where Lucy was living. They ended up in a house in Clonliffe Road which they shared with two others.

Their housemates were witness to violent rows between them and another witness told gardaí that she saw bruises on Sarah Jane's face. No one, especially a woman, could quell the volcanic rage that gripped Mark Nash and his continuing and deepening resentment towards the world which had given him such a raw deal. In June Sarah Jane suffered an even worse emotional blow when her brother Richard died of a drug overdose. She was also pregnant with Nash's child.

This was an added pressure for him, he would now be responsible for the welfare of three children. Sarah Jane wanted to move closer to her family home after her brother's death but Nash disagreed. On August 13, 1997 they argued about the subject on the phone and when Nash arrived home he started shouting at his girlfriend. One of the housemates intervened and he screamed abuse at her, frightening her enough to leave the house that night. Marching upstairs he kicked in the television set and punched the wall. Sarah Jane suggested that they go down the country to her sister Catherine for a break. Sarah Jane hoped that Catherine would be able to help them sort out the difficulties they were having with their relationship. Nash agreed that a change of scene would be a good idea. It was a decision that led to further tragedy for the Doyle family.

Catherine suffered a horrific death and abject terror before she blacked out. Carl suffered less because he had been asleep when he was attacked. Nash lied in evidence saying that Carl was awake but photographs show him in the same position in death as he had been while asleep.

Nash claimed later not to remember what happened. Experts say that this claim is entirely self-serving. Most killers of his kind remember every aspect of their actions, even if they are in a state of alienation where it seems they are onlookers rather than participants in the murder.

From his letters we know the Ripper remembered every detail of his killings, as did the killers of the Clutter family. It is inconceivable that a man who literally ripped a woman apart with a boning knife, inflicting multiple wounds, and who tried to strangle her, would not remember such an act of savagery or indeed the perverted satisfaction he took from it. Nash's contention flies in the face of the knowledge that has been gathered on serial killers of his kind all over the world: they are often of above-average intelligence with perfect recall.

Nash knew enough to realise that he might escape some of the responsibility for his actions if his foul deeds were presented in court as a motiveless crime or the act of a madman. It was yet more proof of Nash's penchant for twisting the truth and his utterly self-absorbed nature that took absolutely no account of the suffering he had caused to the Doyle family, living and dead.

Even though Mark Nash agreed to the trip to Roscommon, there is no reason to believe that the rage, which had resulted in the television being kicked in, would be modified by the country air. The volcano had barely been stoked at the house in Clonliffe Road and experts are in no doubt that Nash's loathsome self-pity had maintained the fire of his rage which could have been ignited by the most innocent of slights, for example, the photograph taken of him as he spilled his insides into the toilet bowl. It was just after that point that his compulsion to kill reached its height.

The results of the toxicology tests in the postmortem found that Carl Doyle had 159 mg of alcohol and cannabis traces in his bloodstream while Catherine had 230 mg. In both cases, the pathologist concluded, this would have induced mild intoxication. On that basis Mark Nash, especially after being sick, could not have been gripped by a drug- and drink-induced hallucinatory paranoia or, on the evidence of the levels of consumption that evening, been anything other than mildly intoxicated.

Apart from his violent rage, he was in command of his senses, allowing him to stab a defenceless woman no less than sixteen times, leaving her with large gaping wounds. This was the frenzied act of a psycho-sexual sadist, who indulgently vented his raging self-pity on two innocent human beings. This is the motive. It is a crime that was identified as far back as the Clutter killings as without *apparent* motive.

It was quite within the defence team's right to attempt to categorise the crime as motiveless and without intent but the prosecution contention was far closer to the mark. That was that Nash stored up his rage against Sarah Jane and used the opportunity of a rural backwater to bludgeon her and kill her sister and brother-in-law in an orgy of bloodletting. Any other explanation, especially his 'being drunk, being sick, seeing a knife and paranoia' simply does not stand scrutiny.

The jury agreed and Mark Nash is serving life, which all experts consulted on this case say should mean exactly life. This is a man with a grudge against life, who will never be satisfied until he kills again and again. The only person that he has any regard for is himself. The dead in his mind are nothing, they may rot but not disturb his peace.

11
THE FANTASIST

Sometime before 5 a.m. on the morning of April 2, 2002 Frank Moynihan, a taxi driver, finished his shift and parked his car at the rear of his mother's house in Dolphin's Barn in Dublin. Walking onto the South Circular Road towards his house in nearby Reuben Street, he noticed smoke coming from a house. As he passed the house he could see flames lapping from an upstairs window over Shazely's butcher's shop.

He ran to a public phone opposite the house and rang the fire brigade. A crew arrived within minutes and fireman Paul McCreevy placed a ladder against the wall and climbed to the first-floor window while the rest of the crew attempted entry through the front. There were flames and smoke coming through a small hole in the window, so McCreevy broke the window and, followed by his colleague Adrian O'Grady who carried a hose, climbed through.

Inside was pitch black and as McCreevy moved around he found one body near a couch and another near the door of the room. The fire was not intense and was put out easily. The firefighters quickly established that the occupants were dead. When they removed their breathing apparatus, they were overcome by the pungent smell of petrol. Shortly afterwards the gardaí arrived at the house and began to examine the scene to try to find the cause of the mysterious fire.

It was quickly established that this was no ordinary domestic accident but, despite exhaustive enquiries and expert technical examination, to this day the origin of the fire has not been found, nor the reason for it. A recent inquest in the Dublin Coroner's Court held an open verdict on the circumstances surrounding the death of the victims, a young woman and a middle-aged man. What cannot be denied is the tragedy of the case, deepened all the more by its strange and disturbing aspects.

The female victim was twenty-three-year-old heroin addict Catherine Dunne from Crumlin, while the man was the tenant of the flat, fifty-one-year-old Joseph Burke. An obese and depressed individual, Burke had the previous evening enticed the young woman to the flat with the promise of a job offer that subsequently proved to be entirely fictitious. They both had sustained only minor burns but died of inhalation of smoke and fire gases.

Catherine's body, fully clothed, was found in a crouching position, face downwards in the middle of the living-room floor while Burke's body, also fully clothed, was lying face upwards with his head jammed against the living-room door. The scene was squalid and chaotic with the small area peppered with garbage, empty packages, the remains of a takeaway and a number of opened and unopened pill packages strewn around.

The back bedroom and bathroom were in equally squalid conditions, which said a lot about the depressed state of the tenant. But the presence of other objects told a lot more about the state of mind and possible intentions of Joseph Burke in advance of inviting Catherine to discuss the 'job offer'. Underneath her lower body were three two-litre plastic milk containers full of petrol. There was another container of petrol beside her right foot and a further one between her body and the fireside hearth. The whole room reeked of petrol. Nearby there was a writing pad with the words 'Catherine' and 'Kathryn' written on it.

In his detailed examination of the scene Garda Technical Bureau expert Detective John Higgins discovered that on the couch there was a pistol, a blank-firing revolver, and, in two locations, sets of keys. Beside one set of keys were two pieces of parcel tape and in another location a part-used roll of parcel tape. All were seemingly innocuous objects but the parcel tape, another section of which was found on the landing, was of particular significance. There was parcel tape found around Catherine's neck and right hand.

This was noted not only by Detective Higgins but also assessed by Deputy State Pathologist Dr Marie Cassidy who in her postmortem concluded that death was due to inhalation of smoke and fire gases, confirming that Catherine Dunne was alive before the fire started.

> One unusual feature was that there appeared to have been tape over her mouth. This appeared to have been in place when the fire started but had come away at some point, presumably when it melted due to the heat, as her tongue was coated in soot.
>
> There was a piece of packing tape across the fingers and the palm of the right hand, between the thumb and the index finger. The tape continued around to the dorsum [back] of the hand where it was still adherent over the knuckles of the index, middle and ring fingers.
>
> She was fully clothed with no injuries to the perineal

area to suggest sexual assault. There was no evidence of any significant marks to the body, apart from small bruises on the upper arm. While they may have preceded the fire, they could have been caused by attempts to drag her from the room.

There were needle marks in both Catherine's arms, suggesting that she was a chronic intravenous drug abuser. Further toxicology analysis showed a moderately high level of methadone.

Catherine's unzipped boots were beside her, as was a pillow suggesting she had been asleep. There was no evidence of third-party involvement so only one person could have been responsible for gripping her and placing the tape on her mouth and wrist, and that was Joseph Burke. But why?

A clue may be found in the rather sad, pathetic and ambiguous nature of the man. He was a balding man with grey hair and beard, unemployed, on disability benefit and dealt in what can only be described as tenth-hand cars which he bought from a scrap dealer and sold on. At fifty-one years of age he was obese and it was found in his postmortem that his heart was enlarged with significant signs of heart disease and blocking of the arteries. He had only one kidney, the other having been removed due to a congenital abnormality. The remaining one was diseased. His liver showed signs of well-established cirrhosis and his blood samples revealed that he was also on anti-depressants. In other words, he was living on borrowed time, suffering from both alcoholism and depression.

According to Anne Dunne, whose brother is married to his sister, he was so self-conscious about his weight that he did not socialise in pubs. Nonetheless he lived in a fantasy world of being a ladies' man and according to the relative was always 'spoofing about some girl or date'. One of his favourite lines was, when phoned, to say that he had been got out of bed, implying there was a woman with him. She wasn't fooled but to try to prove it he would arrive at her house on different occasions with different girls. This was an attempt to reinforce his fantasy version of himself because he may have had to pay for the privilege of female company.

The same relative said another habit he had was going down to Benburb Street to look at the prostitutes, 'looking at the bikes' he called it. 'Looking' was the operative word and if he picked them up it was to impress others. There is little doubt that his physical and mental state would have severely reduced his libido but he persisted in trying to give the opposite impression.

Another obsession was with the Discovery Channel and particularly with a forensic detective series. Inside Joe Burke there was another man trying to break out, a dangerous one. How many times had he watched the re-created murder scenes on Discovery, particularly the programme in which the victim had been taped at the mouth and wrist?

It was in his role as used car dealer that he first met Catherine Dunne just over a year before the fateful night. Her car had been confiscated for tax and insurance violations so she asked him to acquire another banger for her. He brought Catherine and her baby to the relative's house several times but in this case it was turning into an obsession to parallel his other fantasies. He claimed to have given Catherine €1,300 over an eight-month period in 2001.

According to Catherine's boyfriend Derek Weldon, a woman had rung looking for Catherine on Friday, February 26. Presumably Burke had said to Catherine he knew a woman who might be able to give her a job interview.

> On the Friday before Catherine was found in the flat, Vicki [Catherine's friend] got a phone call from a woman looking for Catherine. The woman said that her mother had a beauty salon in Ardee and she was opening one in Dublin herself. She said she was going to Dublin Airport on Friday to go to Paris and she'd be back on Monday and that's when she could interview Catherine.

On Monday, April 1, Catherine rang Joe Burke on his mobile to confirm that the woman was back from Paris. He told her that the woman was delayed. He also told her not to bring her baby Katelyn with her and not to take some of that 'funny stuff' up her nose. An arrangement was made for him to pick her up that evening at her mother's house around 7.30 p.m.

Earlier Burke had rung his in-law Anne Dunne just after 6 p.m. and asked her if she had extra-wide sticky tape as he needed it for a parcel. He pulled up outside her door at 7.20 p.m. There was a woman in the car with him whom she recognised. The previous Saturday he had called and the woman had been with him. He had introduced her as Marie. She was in her mid-thirties with a slim build and dirty blonde hair.

More than likely, she was the person being used to pose as a potential employer for Catherine Dunne. She has never come forward to offer any explanation of Burke's behaviour, which was clearly to entice a young vulnerable addict to his flat on false pretences. After getting the sticking tape, Burke drove away.

When Catherine Dunne was leaving for the 'interview', her boyfriend Derek told her not to be more than two hours. When many hours later there was no sign of her, he rang Burke. It was just after midnight. Burke answered after an interval and said that he had dropped Catherine at the woman's house and left her there. Clearly a blatant lie. Derek was aware of silence in the background. Was it possible that at this stage Burke had taped Catherine's mouth and hands? Nothing less would explain that silence.

This odd and depressive individual was acting out a fantasy probably fuelled by his obsession with *The Forensic Detectives*. A dastardly and misguided ruse to raise his status from the mundaneness of his existence.

Earlier at around 11.30 p.m. Burke's sister Jean had rung him and he complained that she had got him out of bed. Another lie. Another woman rang a half an hour later and he gave her the same false story. What was Catherine Dunne doing all this time?

What Detective Garda Higgins found in his detailed examination of the scene offered more questions than answers. Burke was clothed. The neck of his shirt was open and it, along with his vest, was pulled midway up his chest. There was a disposable cigarette lighter in the breast pocket of his shirt. His trousers had the zip undone. He was wearing socks but no shoes. Catherine Dunne was fully clothed but her black trousers had a side zip which was halfway down. In her upturned hand was an empty packet of John Player Blue.

What can be posited is that the placement of the tape and the presence and placement of the petrol-filled canisters could only have been executed by Burke since there was no evidence of third party involvement. It is patently obvious, from the ruse to get Catherine to his flat and the presence of the petrol containers that he had a plan. In his mind, the unfortunate young woman was essential to his suicidal funeral pyre.

There was no evidence he bore Catherine Dunne ill will or had a grudge and there was never a suggestion of a sexual relationship. So why tape her mouth and wrists and surround her with canisters of petrol other than to fulfil the sick fantasy? Burke knew enough to realise that fire needs ventilation to burn and so he knocked a small hole in the living room window. But his knowledge ended there. By soaking the area with excessive fuel, a real inferno, if that was the intention, was prevented.

One way or another a double death was the clear objective. Tragically a young woman with no suspicion of this was the sacrificial lamb to Burke's destructive fantasy.

The perpetrator taxed the forensic experts to the hilt at the death scene. No source of the ignition of the fire was established and, as lead investigator DI Gabriel O'Hara stated, they could only speculate why the tape was on the body. They did not know how the fire started or why the petrol was present. 'We can't put the matter further,' he concluded.

Joseph Burke's alter ego would have been well pleased. At last, a fantasy fulfilled.

12
A STALKER STRIKES

Raonaid Murray was a vivacious and beautiful seventeen-year-old girl from a middle-class suburb in Dun Laoghaire in south County Dublin. She had, like any teenager, everything to live for, her dreams and expectations, like those of her friends and contemporaries, barely formed. And she had the comfort of a close-knit loving family. The world was her oyster until an autumn night in 1999. There were no shadows over her existence until a stalker struck in the depths of night.

On September 3 Raonaid worked a late-night shift at the Sally West boutique in Dun Laoghaire Shopping Centre where she had a summer job as a junior sales assistant. She finished her shift just after nine that evening and with a colleague crossed the road to Scott's pub. It was Friday night, one for enjoyment, and the girls took a table at the bay window that looked on to the main street, busy with people seeking the pleasure of a good night out.

Scott's pub, patronised mainly by young people, was an ideal drinking spot for her peers, central, open and with no sense of trouble or danger. She was familiar with the surroundings and comfortable in them. There are parts of this suburb where drugs and trouble are expected but this was not one of them. She had spent all her life here and she knew where she was safe and what areas to avoid.

Raonaid made two calls on her friend's mobile to confirm her plans for the night. She was supposed to have been babysitting but this arrangement was cancelled. Such changes of plan acquire extra significance on the heels of fate but they can never take into account the awful recesses of a mind that might take hand or act in that fate. The girls had a few more drinks and at 11.20 p.m. Raonaid left the pub, walked on to the main street and said goodbye to her friend.

Her plan was to go home to change her clothes and pick up some money and then meet other friends at Paparazzi's night club on Marine Road just around the corner towards the ferry terminal and Dart station. It would take her just over fifteen minutes to walk home and on a busy Friday night safety did not seem an issue. It was a warm night and she made her way to the bottom of Corrig Avenue carrying a large Sally West bag and her coat.

With her strawberry blonde hair and confident walk, Raonaid cut a distinctive figure, something that a sick mind might see as a target rather than a source of healthy admiration. As she walked up Corrig Avenue there was someone watching her progress, someone in whom this lovely girl inspired anger and resentment: a reckless and violent risk-taker. He sees her: a young vibrant woman, blonde and attractive, independent and self-assured, just the type of girl he would like to have if he weren't so bound up in his own hang-ups. She is what he wants and can't have. She brings all his social inadequacies into relief. He feels bitter and rejected, inhabiting a world of fantasy where he wreaks revenge on everything he hates, particularly the female form. As he follows her he feels a sense of power, like an animal stalking prey, confident in his superiority. He will confront her and make her feel uncomfortable and then watch as terror makes her dissolve until he is in total command.

At seven minutes to midnight at the top of the avenue Raonaid was spotted by a female motorist, who noticed a young man walking beside her. Her attention was drawn by the fact that the man was acting in an aggressive manner towards Raonaid. She got a further impression that the teenager knew the man and was trying to walk away from him. It might not have struck the witness as particularly unusual. It could have been a lovers' tiff. Such sights are not uncommon on weekend nights and most people know better than to interfere.

That this was not the situation the observer had no way of knowing but the witness did provide a description of the man. He was about 5'10" and aged between twenty-two and twenty-five. He had sandy coloured hair, tossed and unkempt. He was wearing beige combat trousers and a beige sweatshirt or jumper.

Some minutes later Raonaid was seen walking alone as she made her way along Lower Glenageary Road. A short time later a female voice was heard telling someone to 'fuck off'. If this was Raonaid, and it's highly likely that it was, she was being stalked in a dark leafy suburb where there were few people about. In fact, despite the built-up nature of the area, it was perfect ground for a psychotic aggressor, one who knew the area because he was a native, not an interloper, and had rehearsed this scenario in the comfort of his own nearby abode. He was completely comfortable with the geography and knew every nook and cranny of the roads.

Such aggressors are known risk-takers whose compulsion is uppermost in their minds, obviating any thought of being apprehended. This man was on a mission which he had clearly planned in advance by bringing with him an instrument of destruction. He had rehearsed it in his fantasies but this was the crossing point into reality.

In the tree-lined walkway between Silchester Road and Silchester Crescent Raonaid was attacked and stabbed repeatedly with a six-inch kitchen knife. The attacker rammed the knife through the Sally West bag and through her arm and then in a frenzied, crazed manner shoved the knife into her stomach, following this with a violent downwards thrust into her right shoulder, severing an artery. He then fled the scene. Raonaid, her life ebbing away, managed to drag herself a further 100 yards along a grass verge into Silchester Crescent where she died alone.

With a desperate and cruel irony her body was found at 12.40 a.m. by her older sister Sarah who was passing by with a friend. The blood-stained perpetrator returned to his home, which experts and investigators believe was a short distance away.

> Every day of your life you will be haunted by the unspeakable horror of the crime you have committed.
> – *Raonaid's parents addressing*
> *the killer of their daughter.*

Raonaid Murray's parents issued a heartfelt plea on September 4, 2001, the second anniversary of their daughter's murder. The plea was addressed to the killer and also to anyone who might be protecting him. Jim and Deirdre Murray asked mothers, fathers, brothers, sisters or girlfriends who might have information to come forward. If they were unwilling they should examine their conscience.

> By keeping quiet you are allowing Raonaid's murderer
> to walk free.

After one of the biggest murder hunts in the history of the state the killer is still at large. Both investigators and psychologists are convinced that this man has the psyche of a serial killer and will someday be compelled by the unnatural inclination of his mind to kill again. The fact that he has escaped justice will make it all the easier.

Every day he is free young women in particular are at risk and there is no doubt in experts' minds that there is someone protecting him. It is almost certain that he lives within a two-mile radius of the scene of the crime.

The killer's clothes would have been saturated in blood and therefore he could not have travelled far. He would also, in common with such random killers, be in a highly excited and emotional state in the immediate aftermath of the murder.

So what type of person, knowing that the killer had carried out a savage act would willingly protect him and knowingly put other women in danger? Someone, the experts say, with problems possibly of emotional dependence and who have been exposed to the behaviour of the killer over a long period of time. Before addressing this question, it is pertinent to consider a psychological and sexual assessment of the person who is being protected.

Gardaí investigating the brutal murder were supplied with a terrifying profile of the man who they suspect is the killer and the assessment is unequivocal about the possibility of the man killing again. With the help of Dr Art O'Connor and his psychiatric team at the Central Mental Hospital, Dundrum, Dublin, the team believe that the murder was carried out by a young man in his mid-to-late twenties, who 'definitely needs psychiatric help' and is 'obsessed with female dominance and violence'.

There is a definite suspect and investigators have been told by the profile team:

> If he is the killer and there is no action taken against him, he will view this as a sign that he has got away with it and will find it easier to kill again. He is quiet and introverted and also a control freak. He is into nasty or abnormal sex and may have sexual problems in that he cannot perform or suffers from premature ejaculation.
>
> He has had a violent sexual obsession for a considerable time and on the night of the murder this obsession spilled over. There is a possibility that he may have killed animals such as cats in the past. This is significant because there are four people presently in the Central Mental Hospital who killed animals before they committed murder. Two of them killed cats.

The team conclude that if the Garda investigating team are right about the suspect,

> He went out that night armed with a knife to kill. He has long been in the habit of making drawings depicting sexual violence towards women.

During the course of the investigation gardaí came across a number of young men who fit several criteria of the profile. Pornographic material was seized as well as a number of drawings displaying the knifing of female genitalia. The dried blood of a cat was found on the floor of one flat, indicating that the animal had been either killed or tortured.

The psychiatric team suspect that the killer has an interest in martial arts, watches pornographic videos, takes drugs and suffers from depression for which he may have had treatment. Four years after the murder of Raonaid Murray there is only one prime suspect and he is known to have been living no more than ten minutes walk from the scene of the crime. At the time he was a heroin addict and was seen on the night of the murder buying drugs along the route that the victim walked home. He also fitted the description of the witness who said that the young man seen hassling Raonaid at the top of Corrig Avenue had an Oasis-style haircut. There was a further sighting of him shortly after the murder. He was known to carry a knife and had produced it during several altercations. During one row, he stabbed another man.

A source who knew him from the pub and club scene in Dun Laoghaire said that he was known to the victim and had approached her a number of times on social occasions but she had rejected his advances. These rejections provide a motive for his attack, especially at a time when he was in the throes of a disorganised phase in his life, dependent on drugs and suffering from low self-esteem.

While the man has been questioned by investigators of the crime and has no confirmed alibi, witnesses have failed to make a positive facial identification. But there is little doubt that he looked for help to dispose of evidence afterwards and has talked to others about the crime. He still mixes in the pub and social scene in Dun Laoghaire, apparently unphased by the fact that those who mix in these circles are aware of his responsibility for the murder. But he should take account of the fact that it took two decades to trap John Crerar and retribution could be waiting for him around the next corner. Justice sometimes takes its time.

A now-retired highly experienced senior detective who was involved in the investigation commented:

> The savagery of the attack suggests that the killer is psychotic, without inhibition or remorse, and there is no doubt in my mind that, given the opportunity, he will kill again because he is driven by a compulsion to seriously harm and disfigure women. There is someone close to him, whether it be girlfriend or family member, who has had first-hand experience of his cruel behaviour.
>
> It is very frustrating for the Murray family to live with the fact that this killer is roaming the streets – more than likely in their own neighbourhood. It adds immeasurably to their grief as does the knowledge that someone close to this man is protecting him, thus exposing themselves and others to the danger that will never go away. These type of killers do not change their psychological spots, they are a constant threat to both themselves and others. They place no value on life and therefore have no inhibitions about taking it away.

This is in contrast to the emotional turmoil which has engulfed the victim's family from which there is no respite as long as there is no resolution to the case. Such a horrendous blow will always be etched in the collective mind of those closest to Raonaid. What little consolation that could be derived from the abominable act would be in seeing the perpetrator punished.

Their plea to the killer is full of anguish and to his protector it holds more than a hint of desperation, a measure of what has been meted out to them by the very people that they are forced to address:

> Come out from where you are hiding and give yourself up. You will never be able to hide away from what you have done.

> By your silence you are allowing the same thing to happen again. The murderer has struck at the heart of what we hold dear by killing one of our children.

It is tragic that such eloquence born of grief will fall on deaf ears. The killer, assessed by Dr Art O'Connor's team as sexually inadequate with a violent and obsessive hatred of women, has no conscience. It is likely that the protector is as emotionally bankrupt as the killer. And in the majority of cases the killer has power over the protector, a Svengali influence.

13
THE URGE TO CONTROL

According to experts the person most likely to protect the killer is female, who might have suffered abuse, is effectively under his control and may well be terrified of him. Such women are of the classical victim type and might have suffered abuse all their lives but are fatally bound to men who, in effect, perpetuate that status. Because they have never known a proper respectful and loving relationship they have no higher expectations. The men on the other hand are often both physically attractive and cleverly manipulative.

The killer exercises dominance and control and can increase this hold by admitting the crime to the woman and then using the confession to threaten her with implication in it. A notable example in recent times was Rosemary West who, dominated and under the control of her husband Fred, became a willing initiator in the rape, torture and killing of young women. A psychologist who interviewed the female companion of an Australian sex killer said that he had never encountered a more emotionally dependent woman in all his career.

On a simpler level, it is such dependence that explains why women who suffer continual violence and sexual abuse stick with the male perpetrators. Many of these women have been subjected to abuse as children and are caught in a vicious circle. It is very difficult for people with what is termed 'normal' sexual

Mary Jane Kelly, Jack the Ripper's final victim.

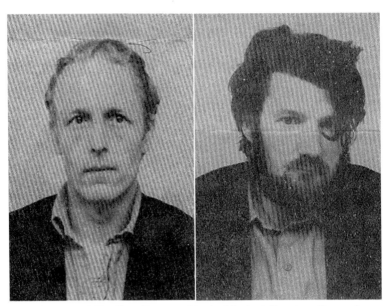

John Shaw and Geoffrey Evans subjected their victims to a litany of depraved torture.

Vinnie Connell, 'a cruel, vicious brute who wreaked havoc in the lives of those he encountered'. (The Irish Times)

Mark Nash lived in a world of celluloid fantasy. (Collins Photo Agency)

Catherine and Carl Doyle: their dream was transformed into a nightmare of blood-letting. (Collins Photo Agency)

Flowers mark the spot where Raonaid Murray's body was found.
(John Minihan)

Phyllis Murphy, victim of a savage attack involving rape and multiple fatal injuries. (Collins Photo Agency)

John Crerar being led into court. (Collins Photo Agency)

John Crerar hides his face but not in shame. Despite overwhelming evidence of his guilt, he continues to maintain his innocence. (Collins Photo Agency)

Jo Jo Dullard, last known to be in a telephone kiosk in the village of Moone, Co Kildare. (Collins Photo Agency)

The disused quarry in Co Kildare to which John Crerar had access.
(John Minihan)

'It's a walking death. There is no closure . . .' John McCarrick holds a photograph of his missing daughter, Annie. (Collins Photo Agency)

Café Java in Leeson Street, Dublin where Annie McCarrick was due in for work the morning after she disappeared. (John Minihan)

Deirdre Jacob, the beautiful eighteen-year-old, was abducted close to her house in broad daylight. (Collins Photo Agency)

Larry Murphy showed no remorse and no pity for the woman he abducted, viciously raped and attempted to murder.
(Collins Photo Agency)

Gerry O'Carroll got the confession of one of Ireland's first serial killers. (John Minihan)

relationships to understand such negative chemistry but it is unfortunately all too common.

One of the most studied relationships in this context is that of Moors murderers Ian Brady and the late Myra Hindley. Between July 1963 and October 1965 they participated in five child murders, some involving sexual assault. Brady, who was in his late twenties when arrested, was a classic control freak and sociopath. He was the illegitimate son of a Glasgow waitress and grew up with no father figure. Raised in a slum in Clydeside, he felt he had got a raw deal in life and from an early age was awash with anger and resentment against society. Brady was going to put his name on the map with letters of blood.

He moved to Manchester in 1954 with his mother and stepfather. After spending time in a borstal for petty crime, he got a job as stock clerk in a chemical firm. He was twenty-one and became obsessed with Nazi history and literature and the writings of the Marquis De Sade.

Brady, despite his unhealthy obsessions, was clever, intelligent and his sullen demeanour proved highly attractive to the opposite sex. When he was twenty-three, an eighteen-year-old typist joined the office. Myra Hindley was from a conservative Catholic background with a penchant for dyed blonde hair and bright red lipstick. She was bowled over by Brady who, the essence of cool at the time, dressed in black and rode a motorbike.

Hindley fell madly in love with Brady who quickly took control of his naive girlfriend. She became in time an adjunct to his massive ego and a participant in his perverted sexual practices. In effect she became his sex slave: men like Brady are not interested in normal sex or its role as an expression of affection.

In her confession she said that in the beginning of the courtship Brady took a lot of interest in her sexually and they had normal intercourse. But soon he seemed to be only interested in pleasuring himself, at times just wanting masturbation. A number of times he forced her to have anal sex which she found incredibly painful. Then he got her to insert a candle up his anus while he masturbated. This amounted to the contemptuous sexual use of a woman: all she was good for was servicing his deviant sexual needs, to translate his fantasies. In common with his kind, it expressed a basic hatred of women, thus his sodomising – the more pain for her, the more pleasure for him.

Psychologists have found that women in such relationships have, despite being subjected to such abuse, a higher emotional dependency than women in more conventional relationships. Hindley confirmed this in her confession saying that, in spite of the deviant sex and the humiliation, she was still besotted with Brady. She did, however, find this feeling difficult to explain.

Brady, and men like him, draw women into a fantasy world of achievement. The women are seduced by an imaginary world created by the compulsive lying of their men. These sex killers are incapable of telling the truth because of their tenuous hold on reality. It was the measure of his power over Hindley that Brady made her a willing accomplice in the murder of children.

Pornography seems to play a vital role in the minds of such killers and is constantly referred to by psychiatrists and profilers as a common indulgence. Brady used a time-lapse camera to take pornographic photographs of himself and Hindley engaged in sexual activity, some showing sexual intercourse with the wearing of hoods. From Jack the Ripper on, sexual perversion is a stock in trade of the serial killer and someone other than the victims, with rare exceptions, has been subjected to their dark sexual taste.

After three of the murders, on St Stephen's day 1965, the pair picked up ten-year-old Lesley Ann Downey at a fairground. They brought the child back to Hindley's grandmother's house, her grandmother being away at the time. They took pornographic photographs of the girl and tape-recorded her screams for mercy before Brady raped and strangled her. They later buried her body on the moors.

Brady claimed later that Hindley actively participated in the murders, while she countered by saying he always did the killing when she was in a car or waiting in another room. What is not in dispute, as in the Rosemary West case, is that she was entirely complicit in the appalling acts of savage indulgence. Wherever they were, both these women protected the killer and those who protect are equally culpable.

There are exceptions. Sonia Sutcliffe, wife of the Yorkshire Ripper Peter Sutcliffe, won a lot of money in damages from the media that suggested she must have known something of her husband's activities. He was responsible for thirteen murders of women between 1975 and 1980 but his wife had no idea of his nocturnal killings which were mainly but not exclusively of prostitutes. There are some sex and psychopathic killers who keep the swirling sewer of their minds to themselves, surprising everyone when they have been caught, even those closest to them.

This is because these killers can be placed in certain

psychological categories. Some are complete loners, while others have some basic social skills. Limited as they are, these skills allow them to have relationships which seem on the surface to conform to the accepted norm. The categories are divided into two by FBI profilers under the heading lust killer. Twenty years after the analysis of the Clutter killers, Hickock and Smith, two agents at the FBI Behavioural Science Unit at Quantico, Roy Hazelwood and John Douglas, defined the lust killer and the impact of his work. Such murder they describe as:

> One of the most heinous crimes committed by man.
> While not a common occurrence, it is one that frightens and arouses the public as does no other crime.

The lust murder they say is unique and distinguished from other cruel killing by the involvement of mutilation – displacement of breasts, genitals or rectum. While there are rare exceptions, basically two types of individuals commit the murder: the organised nonsocial and the disorganised asocial personalities.

The first personality is egocentric, dislikes people generally but can play a social role giving an entirely different impression of himself to other people. But behind the mask is a cunning, methodical killer who is very much aware of the impact of his work on society. He likes to shock and offend because it gives him a certain power and status that he does not have in his ordinary life. He lives a good distance away from the crime scene and will move about to attain his objectives.

Like the disorganised asocial, the organised nonsocial killer harbours a deep-seated hatred for people, which he expresses by the aggressive and seemingly senseless acts of violence. This hostility would have first manifested in adolescence. He is a troublemaker and manipulator and totally self-centred. It is his aim to get even with society for some perceived wrongdoing against him and this he achieves by inflicting pain, terror and punishment on others.

The disorganised asocial killer is a loner who has difficulties in having interpersonal relationships and consequently feels rejected and lonely. He lacks the cunning of his opposite number and commits the crimes in a frenzied and less ordered manner. The crime is likely to be committed relatively close to where he lives or works, where he feels more at ease. Family and co-workers would describe him as a nice, quiet person who likes to keep himself to himself but who has never quite achieved his potential. During adolescence he may have engaged in voyeuristic activities and the theft of women's clothing. These activities serve as a substitute for his inability to approach, engage and get on with women on a one-to-one basis.

The state of the crime scene gives a clue to which type of killer was involved. This includes the presence or absence of the murder weapon, the location of the body – whether it was left at the scene or moved to another place after the murder – and also the sequence in which certain acts of violence were performed.

According to the FBI experts:

> Typically, the asocial killer leaves the body at the scene of death and, while the location may not be open to the casual observer, there is no attempt to conceal the

body. Conversely the nonsocial killer commits the murder in a secluded or isolated area and may transport it to another area where it is likely to be found. While there is no intention of being caught, the nonsocial type wants the excitement derived from publicity about the body's discovery and the impact on the community.

They say that the killers usually murder their victims quickly after abduction or attack. If there is evidence of torture or mutilation prior to death, the perpetrator is adjudged as the nonsocial type. They rarely use a gun for murder, as it is considered too impersonal a weapon for a sexually sadistic murderer. To attain the high they seek in the fulfilment of their fantasy-inspired killing, they prefer to be more directly involved in the violence.

Most frequently deaths result from strangulation, blunt force or the use of a sharp, pointed instrument such as a knife. The asocial type is more prone to using a weapon of opportunity and may leave it at the scene, while the nonsocial type may carry the murder weapon with him and take it away from the scene of the crime. Therefore the murderer's choice of weapon and proximity to the scene can be greatly significant in the investigation.

The study of the mind of psycho killers, what makes them and where they come from has also progressed since the Clutter murders although, despite the sophistication of the methods applied, the basic principles remain constant. And it is not as complicated as the horror of the crimes committed may suggest. As one forensic psychiatrist put it to me,

> The psychopath is alarmingly simple: he sees everything in black and white. Once a thought enters his mind, he follows it through without the restraint, examination and inhibition that most of us would apply. Because he is usually suffused with self-pity and sees the world as being against him, he has no remorse for his actions. Many explain their actions by saying that something or someone was 'wrecking their head'.

The psychiatrist explained that, in computer terms, the psycho killer's hard drive is the same as the rest of us but the software is different. The assessment of a highly dangerous American psychopath, Cameron Hooker, expresses this in slightly different terminology but the conclusion is the same:

> People like to believe in Einstein or Beethoven – geniuses – but they hate to believe in their opposites. A genius is a mutant, something unnatural. But just as some people are born with extra intelligence, others are born without much intelligence or without fingers, limbs or consciences. The human body is phenomenally complex, with trillions of cells, and trillions of things can go wrong. Cameron Hooker is a fluke, an accident of internal wiring. His instincts are the opposite of yours and mine.

The accident of internal wiring can be accommodated and enhanced by background, parenthood or lack of it, and the circumstances of childhood experience. It is not just a matter of being born under a bad sign, after all every newborn child is brought into the world in a state of total dependency and innocence. It is what happens afterwards that all kinds of research shows is what matters.

Quantico research, including interviews with numerous killers, clearly demonstrates that family circumstances play a crucial part in determining the actions of an individual both in later childhood and adulthood. In the case of many killers, there was a high degree of instability, deprivation, a hostile or poor relationship with the father, and physical or sexual abuse in childhood and teens.

An absent father figure and an overweening, pampering and dominating mother figure may also spell danger for the child's development as was demonstrated in the case of Vinnie Connell. Depending on the degree of separation in the parenting roles and the intensity and circumstances of the unbalanced relationship, catastrophic results can ensue. The breakdown of family ties, the absence of the normal, loving and tactile relationship, turns the fledgling killers into self-centered, self-obsessed loners.

These children become highly sexed in advance of their peers and initiate sex games with girls at school. This is where the emphasis on sex begins and then slowly transforms into perversion. Most experts in the area believe that fantasy is the foundation for the development of sexual perversion. Since the fantasist is ashamed of the nature of his autoerotic thoughts he tends to avoid too much contact with reality, preferring to spend as much time in the dream world inside his own head, indulging and developing those fantasies.

They blame their own failed circumstances on the world and their response to the physical or sexual abuse suffered within their families is to inflict it on others. As they grow, their fantasies grow increasingly violent, and they sometimes start by torturing and killing animals and domestic pets before graduating to humans. They become obsessed with pornography and their preferred form of sexual activity is masturbation as they are unable to establish contact with the opposite sex.

Their unnatural fantasies and stimulation by pornography ultimately demand a translation from fantasy to the real world and therein lies its danger. The masturbatory fantasies are fuelled by Peeping Tom activities, stalking, looking and then progressing to sexual assault and ultimately murder.

Eventually the situation will arise that prompts the dreamer to come out of the fantasy world and translate his thoughts into a horrendous reality with an act of violence. This gives him the sense of being powerful, in control and alive. Murder is a way of giving him a new and welcome sense of self-worth, for the dreamer is full of self-pity and paralysed by low self-esteem. And yet that low self-esteem is often well hidden by a charming and confident exterior that can be attractive to women. Under that exterior, there is a raging spark that like a volcano will suddenly erupt without a hint of warning. This will be the result of years of disaffection and fantasy and the sudden and overwhelming desire to control in the only way possible – by force. This lust or sex murder is ironically not driven by a sexual impulse but by power and the urge to control.

The absence of a father figure seems to be a common factor in the genesis of serial killers. One of the most notorious killers in US history, Ted Bundy, estimated to have killed between twenty-nine and thirty-four women, was an illegitimate child born to a respectable secretary in a home for unmarried mothers. Significantly, his mother always refused to disclose the identity of the father, a factor not conducive to a healthy sense of identity for her boy.

Bundy was left in the home for a while and then brought to his grandfather, a despotic man, who beat up his wife but doted on his grandson. His mother moved town when he was four and he was devastated to lose the only father figure he had ever known. His mother subsequently married but he never succeeded in establishing a relationship with his stepfather.

To compensate for his lack of any solid identity, as a schoolboy he was a fantasist, dreaming of being adopted by the cowboy star Roy Rogers. He became an inveterate liar, another strait of such killers, gripped constantly as they are by unremitting self-delusion. Bundy wanted to be 'somebody' but his streak of self-pity prevented him from ever being a success. Again Bundy was very good-looking and attractive to the opposite sex.

Despite his hatred of women, probably initially inspired by his mother, he had a huge sex drive, being a compulsive masturbator from an early age and indulging in bondage with his girlfriends, while fantasising about necrophilia. On the outside, his male friends were envious of his confidence, charm and good looks but the early frustrations of his life left him convinced that he was going to be a loser. He became a compulsive thief and later transferred this compulsion to rape and murder.

Bundy, like a spoiled child, was taking what the world did not give freely to him. This activity developed to a huge degree of indulgence, which on the surface might seem to have been some form of insanity, but when stripped to its basics was a planned and calculated form of ghastly wickedness. Bundy's risk-taking in his robbing and killing was a form of suicidal behaviour, another trait deeply embedded in the serial killer's psyche.

While a lot of killers are so deluded and trapped by their fantasies that they would be hard put to explain the real motivations of their actions, some others are compelled to write about their experience to in some way offer an explanation. American psychotic Albert Brust was one of those. He kept a journal that provided a graphic expression of the negative, depressed and morbid personality of his kind.

> My reason tells me that I have nothing to live for. Intellectually, sexually, occupationally, socially – everywhere a dead end.

His writings, he explained, had a tranquillising effect on him, reinforcing the Dr Jekyll side of his personality. But, he wrote,

> It is also true that they paralyse me into inaction. They cause me to think about death, to be fatalistic and pessimistic, prone to suicide. The culprit is my emotions. Once stirred, blind rage tends to take over and I get both homicidal and suicidal.

Many killers, as well as being prone to depression, are inclined to be heavy drinkers and drug users which, far from providing an escape from their morbid thoughts, only tends to fuel the effect of their demons. Dennis Nilsen the British homosexual serial killer summed it up in his confession after his arrest:

> God only knows what thoughts go through my mind when it is captive within a destructive binge. Maybe the cunning, stalking, killer instinct is the only single concentration released from a mind which in that state knows no morality . . . There is no disputing the fact that I am a violent killer under certain circumstances. It amazes me that I have no tears for these victims. I have no tears for myself or for those bereaved by my actions. Am I a wicked person, constantly under pressure, who just cannot cope with it, who escapes to wreak revenge against society through a haze of a bottle of spirits?

Rarely outside the psychological and profiling arena of expertise has the mind of the serial killer been so accurately and articulately described. What is most striking and dramatic is how easily the killer can distance himself from his actions and his victims and the implications of what he has done. It is almost as if he is speaking about himself in the third person – a spectator of the horror, with no emotional connection and no remorse. He has no tears for the victims or their relatives. A man who has murdered, who has had sexual relations with the corpses and then dismembered them in the crudest of fashions, feels nothing. That is the human animal we are dealing with, one who is immune to feeling, one who abducts, rapes, murders and buries and then moves on without a thought or a glance backwards.

One thing psychopathic killers have learnt over the years is that the best chance of not getting caught is to get rid of the greatest receptacle of evidence – the body. Not many have managed to do this with any degree of success, except in Ireland. That success has been mostly in east Leinster and has also been, by international standards and given the small geographical area, phenomenal.

14
A VILE ACT

There is no time of the year when death does not have an impact. In every season there is a poignant reminder whether it be the burgeoning promise of spring, the bright careless days of summer or the golden brown of autumn. Winter has its own resonance, especially for the old, as it is the season of darkness, closest to parting from this life. But in the depths of that season Christmas is the most traumatic because it is normally a time for joyous celebration and the tying of familial bonds.

It was Christmas 1979 and a young woman was looking forward to the festive season in Kildare in the usual way: buying presents, having a good time and being in the bosom of her direct and extended family. Ordinary but nonetheless exciting expectation. The New Year would bring whatever it may, but the now was for the now, warm feelings were all, and the cold that enveloped the land did not matter.

Philomena Murphy, known to all as Phyllis, was the third youngest of a family of ten. Her father was an army man and she grew up in Kildare town. When she was seven her mother died and afterwards she formed a close bond with the Martins, a family who lived next door. They moved to Newbridge in 1969. In 1978 Phyllis moved to stay with the Martins' grandmother in Rathangan.

Phyllis was known as a shy, reserved young woman who loved dancing. After her Inter Cert she worked in a number of local knitwear factories as a cutter. She was totally family orientated who liked nothing more than to baby-sit the children of her brother and sisters.

On December 22 of 1979 Phyllis, now twenty-three years of age, went shopping in Newbridge where she lived in digs with the Martin family. At 3 p.m. she visited a hairdressers where she got her hair permed in an Afro style and returned to her digs to wrap Christmas gifts. She then called to her brother Gerard who lived doors away, and afterwards went to see her best friend Barbara Luker to make an arrangement to meet later that evening in Kildare where she intended to spend the night with her family.

Having left Barbara, she made her way to the stop outside the Keadeen Hotel where she intended to get the 6.50 p.m. bus to Kildare. While she was waiting a car pulled up and a man she knew offered her a lift. It could have been a chance encounter but this man had other things in his mind for a long time before. When later her friend Barbara turned up in Kildare at the appointed time, there was no sign of Phyllis. Barbara contacted the family and there was immediate worry because Phyllis was punctilious and not a person who would, without notice, break an appointment.

The gardaí were contacted but as one day followed another, fears grew for her safety. Throughout Christmas and afterwards, the search spread from Kildare out onto the Curragh plains. The gardaí knew that a murder investigation was under way, as a number of clothing items belonging to the missing woman were found at Colgan's Cut on the Curragh, including boots and a cardigan. Days later, mittens and the belt of a coat were recovered. But there was no sign of Phyllis Murphy. The search progressed slowly and frustratingly. The worst was feared but the worst was yet to be found.

It can only be imagined what a desperate and agonising time it was for the family. Christmas had been destroyed and each minute and hour that passed was an eternity, the lack of resolution turning the screw of pain and loss. As time passes there is a certain acceptance of the inevitable. After that a body is a consolation. It would be a consolation denied many families in the decades that followed but not the Murphys.

At the same time the killer enjoyed the Yuletide and its aftermath, mixing with friends, relations and family. He possibly, as is his type, revelled in the distant notoriety, confident that he would never be connected with the disappearance particularly as he had been clever enough to cover his tracks. He could have done a lot more to conceal the evidence but, next time, he would be more careful and less impulsive.

The temperature was freezing in January, inclement for the living but curiously comforting, in the end, for the relations of the dead. Irony is something that can cross all borders. In the close to sub-zero temperature of January 18, 1980 the naked body of a young woman was found lying face upwards under a canopy of trees, one arm resting over her stomach. The Garda search party stumbled across the gruesome discovery near Turlough Hill along the Wicklow Gap, a remote and forbidding spot in the depths of winter.

The body had been only partially concealed with a number of branches which had been blown away by the winds that sweep across that semi-mountainous region. It was an indication that the killer had been in a hurry. At that time of the year, in that terrain, he would have had no problem burying the body properly without the least fear of interruption. There must have been some pressing need for him to leave in such a hurry.

The crime scene was set up and preserved and the investigators awaited the arrival of Dr John Harbison, the State Pathologist, and the forensic team. Anything at a crime scene can provide a clue but the body is considered by experts as a crime scene in itself. While forensics is a highly skilled discipline, what is being sought is quite simple.

Where a crime involves violence, the people involved come into close contact and there is a transfer of a variety of materials from one to another. This is called Locard's Exchange Principle and is the basis of crime scene analysis: what was left behind, what was taken away, what was exchanged, be it fibre, skin or bodily fluid. Find it and the murder may be solved. In this shocking killing, that principle would prove to be vital.

It was quickly established the body was that of Phyllis Murphy and the savage nature of her killing was immediately obvious. The pathologist found twenty-five separate injuries to her body, mainly concentrated in the areas of face, neck and head. Experienced murder squad personnel were shocked by the extent of the violence and the suffering and terror they knew the victim would have suffered. She had been strangled and bruises to the inner part of her thighs indicated that her legs had been forced apart in the act of rape. The earlier discovery of some of the victim's clothing in Colgan's Cut indicated that Phyllis had been attacked at that spot, raped and murdered. Her body had then been transported by car to the remote spot over twenty miles from the first scene and dumped with a hurried effort to conceal it. The rest of her clothes had been taken away by the killer. At nearby Lockstown Upper an elderly couple on their way to Mass the day after Phyllis disappeared saw flames from a small fire on the roadside. In the follow-up investigation a button from Phyllis's Lois jeans, the metal fasteners from her bra and the burnt tweed of her overcoat were among the fire's remains.

Clearly this killer was intent on destroying evidence that might in any way link him to the crime and also demonstrated that he had, whatever his profession, a certain forensic awareness by dumping the body many miles from the real murder scene. He knew that the longer the delay in finding the body, the less likely there would be any evidence left to connect him to the crime. However, he was frenzied and careless enough to leave items of clothing at the first scene. Instead of distancing himself from the murder location he had brought himself closer. But it was the only thing he had left to chance.

Despite the time lapse during which such evidence might deteriorate in quality or disappear altogether, vaginal swabs were taken to collect potential traces of semen. It was four years before the application of DNA fingerprinting to forensic science but semen, if present, could provide vital evidence through blood-type analysis. It seemed, however, unlikely.

But there was an important factor that favoured the collection of forensic evidence. The body had lain in freezing cold for four weeks. The rate of postmortem changes and decomposition are considerably slowed in such low ambient temperature. Had it been the height of summer there would have been little or no evidence left to preserve.

It was also before the science of psychological profiling had been developed but the murder investigators had a very clear mental picture of a particularly vicious, cold-blooded individual who risked everything for a sadistic sex killing. The brute force employed with the use of a blunt instrument was that perpetrated by a strong, relatively young man.

'I couldn't believe it when I saw the body,' recalled the now-retired head of the Murder Squad, John Courtney. 'He gave her a terrible battering. I had never seen the likes.'

Under the normal progress of a murder investigation, this should have been straightforward given, as well as the basic detective work, a little bit of luck, the break that most murder hunts need. But instead it was to take a most extraordinary journey and looked set to join the annals of unsolved murders in Ireland.

In the course of the investigation that followed, over 2,000 statements were taken and the suspect list stretched to no less than 600 names. A number of blood samples were taken from a selection of suspects to see if they matched with blood found on the body.

Ten days into the enquiry an ex-army man by the name of John Crerar was questioned. He voluntarily gave a blood sample some months later which did not match any blood on the body and he had a cast-iron alibi. He was eliminated. The investigation dragged on with hope of a result fading as each day passed.

A new inquiry was launched a year later but still there was no advance in finding the killer. The odds were that the perpetrator was going to get away with murder. Because of the sexual and sadistic nature of the crime it was also likely that the killer would strike again and would be more careful about both the circumstances of the abduction and particularly the disposal of the body. But there was nothing the investigating team could do. They had some, what then seemed flimsy, evidence and nobody with which to match it.

But there was, in the years before the discovery of genetic fingerprinting, also a scientific problem which inhibited greatly the success of the enquiry. At the State Laboratory attempts to isolate a blood grouping from enzymes in the semen found in Phyllis Murphy's body failed. Along with blood-stain cards from fifty-one other suspects, Crerar's blood stain as well as swabs taken from the body were returned to the exhibits officer for this case.

The swabs were in narrow plastic tubes, meticulously labelled by Detective Inspector Colm Dardis. The blood-stain cards were individually packaged and stored back to back. Garda Christy Sheridan put them in a steel locker at Naas Garda Station and kept the sole key.

In 1988 Naas Garda Station was moved to a new location and the contents were also moved. On December 20, 1988, almost nine years to the day after the murder, Garda Sheridan handed the exhibits over to the superintendent's clerk Garda Finbar McPaul, who locked them in another cabinet in Kildare station.

For a crime that had effectively gone cold, this was meticulous and responsible preservation of evidence. This seemingly routine piece of housekeeping would prove highly significant – but not for a very long time. Meanwhile, the victim, the case and the killer were lost and forgotten in the public consciousness.

In the interim there was a discovery that would advance forensic science almost beyond recognition and which would eventually be responsible for catching and convicting Phyllis Murphy's killer. A British geneticist, Alec Jeffreys, developed a technique known as DNA fingerprinting. It was based on the theory that everyone has a unique genetic make-up and an individual's cells contain a copy of that individual's genetic blue-print.

Advances in genetics in the seventies had been applied to detect variation in DNA between individuals. While it is a fact that 99.8% of a person's DNA is the same as everyone else's, the remaining fraction is hugely different. In 1984 Professor Jeffreys of Leicester University made the quantum leap by developing a method of identifying individual differences in DNA. He discovered that, within the highly variable regions of DNA, there are repeating sequences of bases. The number of repeats can vary enormously from one individual to the next and the chance that it is the same as another person's stretches into the region of billions. He realised that if he could find a way of counting the number of repeats, he would have a unique genetic signature for each individual.

He designed specific enzyme probes that could attach to these sections of DNA repeats. The probes were radioactively labelled so that wherever they bonded to DNA there would be radioactive emissions. The DNA was then exposed to X-ray film to provide an image of dark bands, different for each individual.

The first practical application came when police in Leicester approached Jeffreys to help solve the double murder of two young women. Jeffrey's team was able to extract a DNA fingerprint from a tiny semen sample taken from the scene of the crime. Blood samples were taken from almost 4,000 local men and, in one, they found an exact match to the DNA collected at the crime scene. This led to a successful prosecution and conviction in 1987.

A later development to this science would also prove vital in the Phyllis Murphy case. The Polymerase Chain Reaction (PCR) technique can single out small and degraded samples of DNA and copy them millions of times to provide a large enough sample for identification.

In July 1997 the locker in Kildare station was opened and the contents handed to Detective Inspector Brendan McArdle. The inspector had taken more than a keen interest in DNA and was surprised at the excellent state of the contents.

'To my astonishment the critical exhibits were there, packed, properly marked and appeared to be in a good state,' he recalled.

The initial analysis was carried out by Dr Maureen Smith and Dr Louise McKenna at the State Laboratory and then sent to a laboratory in Britain for further advanced testing. A DNA fingerprint was found in the semen sample taken from the body of the victim. A match was found in one of the blood-stain cards taken from suspects. The match pointed out John Crerar as the killer.

He was arrested on July 13, 1999 and taken in for questioning. Still confident of getting way with the murder he offered a fresh blood sample which served to confirm without a shadow of a doubt that the investigators had finally got their man.

Operation Trace had by now been set up and personnel and resources were utilised to review the original investigation file. Gardaí realised that Crerar had gone to great lengths to cover up his involvement in the murder. He had washed out the boot of his car with boiling water and asked garage owner John Dempsey to say that he had delivered his Datsun car to him for repairs at 7 p.m. on December 22. Dempsey refused. It also became clear that, with the DNA link confirming him as the rapist, Crerar must have persuaded colleagues to provide him with an alibi. The investigators could see that this man had tried to cover all angles. As careful and manipulative as he was, he could not have been in two places at the one time.

Crerar had been working as a security guard at the Black and Decker site in Kildare at the time of the murder. Two colleagues had provided an alibi. Former army mate and near-neighbour, Paddy Bolger, told gardaí that Crerar had turned up for work shortly after 8 p.m. and another guard on the site, Jim Mahoney, confirmed this. He saw a car coming onto the site around 8 p.m. and was fairly sure that it was driven by Crerar.

But, confronted by the new and incontrovertible evidence of the Operation Trace team, Bolger admitted that he had lied for Crerar. In fact Crerar did not turn up until at least 8.40 p.m and left straight away, not returning until 10.45 p.m., giving him more than enough time to drive to Wicklow and dispose of the body. Mahoney admitted that he had also lied. Albeit twenty years on, the case was complete. John Crerar was charged with the murder of Phyllis Murphy. Still confident that he would not be caught, Crerar agreed to give a fresh sample. While never admitting any involvement in the murder the prime suspect was, in scientific terms, signing his confession – in blood.

There are many cases in which justice is hard won and which take time but two decades on places this case in a league of its own.

The important thing was that when the break eventually came there were investigators of the highest integrity and calibre able to grasp the opportunity. They were first the keeper of the original samples and DI Brendan McArdle.

> I lecture on homicidal death of women and children and have to keep up with advances in all aspects of my job and particularly advances like the PCR technique which ensures that DNA taken from the most minute sample is suitable for analysis. Prior to this, the samples we had in the Phyllis Murphy case were too small to produce an acceptable sample that would stand up to the test of proof in a court.
>
> Back at the start of the case we were in a situation where it would not be solved unless the killer walked into the station and gave himself up. I did not know, when the case was reopened in 1997, if the swabs were still in existence and, if they were, had the samples deteriorated over the long passage of time. I was directed to Finbar McPaul the superintendent's clerk in Kildare. He had the files and he also had a sealed package at the office which held the vital evidence. What was critical were the swabs and the skin cards with blood but we had nothing with which to compare them.

DI McArdle took the samples away and five days later handed them over to Dr Maureen Smith in the State Laboratory. In January 1998 she got back to the investigator and informed him that nine swabs of semen recovered out of seventeen were capable of being analysed.

> We knew that there was a good forensic laboratory in Abingdon in England. I made contact with Matthew Greenhall and in March of that year I travelled over and handed him the nine swabs. The following month he told us that he had the full DNA profile, from the semen traces left in the body, of the man who had raped Phyllis Murphy.

It was a huge breakthrough and the next step was to go back over the files of the men interviewed and who had given samples. The Assistant Commissioner gave the resources to formally begin the investigation. The forty-eight stain cards were brought to Abingdon and one of them was found to provide a blood match with the DNA from the semen sample. In July a team was set up under Detective Superintendent Sean Camon and the entire murder file was reopened. One of the things that worried DI McArdle and the team was that, after twenty years, witnesses or suspects could have left the country or died.

> It was strange but everyone involved back in 1979 was alive and well and all more or less in the same location. Most witnesses had given statements, so we reviewed them and sorted out which ones were relevant and then exposed the false alibi which had in effect prevented the progress of the case for all that time.

On October 31, 2002, almost twenty-three years after the killing,

John Crerar was found guilty by a unanimous verdict of the murder of Phyllis Murphy on December 22, 1979. Throughout the trial the father of five, whose wife had been pregnant at the time of the murder, was stony-faced and showed no trace of emotion. The evidence of State Pathologist Dr John Harbison, when he described the extent of the injuries to the victim, caused Phyllis Murphy's family to leave the court to avoid being upset. There were twenty-five injuries to the body including multiple abrasions indicating a frenzied and merciless attack. Dr Harbison said that death was due to manual strangulation and that bruising on the inside of the thighs 'was consistent with the forcible parting of the legs, in other words with an attempt to rape.'

Despite DNA evidence and being caught weaving a web of lies and deceit around his movements on the night of the murder, Crerar continued to maintain his innocence throughout the trial.

Why should he do this in the face of such overwhelming evidence? Self-preservation? But from what? Hoping that an appeal might work? Or is it possible that this killer, whose merciless treatment of his young victim has all the hallmarks of a sexual psychopath, had a lot more to hide than this murder?

15
A MAN WITH A HISTORY

What is utterly clear from the experience of Phyllis Murphy's murder is that Crerar is a manipulative liar and that any alibi he might offer in relation to other abductions cannot be trusted.

DI Brendan McArdle believes that the abduction, rape and murder of Phyllis Murphy was not a once-off crime. 'I do not believe that he committed this murder and then stopped,' he says. As profilers have pointed out in relation to other cases of similar killers, there is usually a history of either stalking or sexual assault before the murder.

Crerar is believed by investigators to have been responsible for a number of serious sexual assaults and at least one rape, all of which went unreported because the victims were afraid. One woman told gardaí that she had been raped by the former army sergeant but was too frightened to press charges.

Crerar was known all his life as a serial predator who, as a soldier in his twenties, was alleged to have abused two children. He was never charged with those offences but the victims have never withdrawn the allegations. The abuse allegation emerged during the investigation into the murder of Phyllis Murphy.

Local sergeant Kevin Derrane was placed in charge of questionnaires for Kildare town early in 1980 and is believed to have come across the abuse allegation while carrying out door-to-door enquiries. When he questioned Crerar he made a note on top of the questionnaire recommending that this man's story be checked. Three statements containing allegations of abuse and sexual assault were taken by gardaí as a result of Derrane's alert.

They were taken two days before January 16, 1980 when Crerar was asked to make a detailed statement about his movements on the night that Phyllis Murphy went missing. At the time of making the statements, the first woman was a minor, but the second was over eighteen and has since confirmed that she has never withdrawn the allegation.

When questioned about these allegations Crerar claimed that the victim was a liar. He said that when she was a teenager he had caught her stealing and that she had come on to him to get out of the situation. There may have been some kissing and feeling going on, he claimed, but that was only because the girl had come on to him.

The 1980 statements tell a different story which, in the light of subsequent events, have to carry more credibility than the word of a convicted rapist and murderer. One woman recalls that when she was ten years of age Crerar enticed her into a caravan where he then lived, claiming his wife wanted to see her. He then locked the door, took off her pants and placed a newspaper under her body. He proceeded to seriously sexually assault her. The girl was further abused when she was fifteen. She said that Crerar would give her money to keep quiet and 'would get a bit mad when I wouldn't let him go the whole way'. She never consented to any of the abuse, but she was afraid of him, a reaction that this monster engendered in most females.

The statement of another alleged victim said that he tried to sexually assault her in her own home but that she picked up a knife and threatened to stick it in him if he did not back off. A third statement from a woman alleged that Crerar molested her from the time she was eleven. She alleged that one night while she was babysitting at his house in Woodside, she awoke to find him 'touching my body all over. I told him to go away or I would scream and wake up his wife.'

In the same year as the murder Crerar was the prime suspect for a sexual assault in the artillery officers' mess. Then a DJ at a dance in the mess, Crerar was seen by army colleagues going upstairs where a time later a woman was violently and indecently assaulted. Her cries for help were heard and the attacker ran off, jumping from a bedroom balcony to escape. The woman was not able to identify her attacker but investigators found a large dent in the roof of a car which was parked directly underneath the balcony. Crerar was noted to be limping later on. He was the prime suspect but there was insufficient evidence to bring charges. The incident and his believed connection with it did however put him on the suspects' list for the murder of Phyllis Murphy.

It is widely accepted by experts that such a history is common among psychopathic killers and it is only a matter of time until there is a graduation from sexual assault to rape and eventually murder. This is precisely the journey travelled by John Crerar and it is one that may not have stopped after the murder of Phyllis Murphy. Despite the delay in bringing him to justice most people in the area suspected him of involvement and many women were terrified by his presence or his attentions.

One such woman lived in the vicinity of the Aga Khan stud where, she said, Crerar once worked in a security guard capacity.

He used to drive by here regularly. Most women in the area were terrified of him because of his reputation and the fact that he was known as the prime suspect for the murder of Phyllis Murphy. There is a disused quarry at the back of the stud and I saw him going in there on many occasions.

It was sometime around midnight and I saw the vehicle that he drove at the time, parked outside the gates of the quarry. The headlights were on and the gates were slightly ajar. He must have been in the quarry. It sent a shiver up my spine because it was the night after Jo Jo Dullard had disappeared from Moone village. I told a friend but we were too scared to do anything about it. Some time later my friend did report it to the gardaí but the quarry was never searched.

The woman claims to have seen Crerar on at least half a dozen occasions on the grounds of the quarry, which is now completely overgrown by grass and bushes. He had access to the land because it was owned by the Aga Khan. On a number of occasions, Crerar was seen to be lighting a bonfire and on others he was digging. While it was utilised for the dumping of waste, there was no question of animals or horses being buried in the quarry.

On one occasion he was seen just inside the gates of the quarry arguing with a fresh-faced young man. Having seen pictures of Larry Murphy the witness says that he bears a strong resemblance to the man she saw with Crerar.

Another witness from the locality who does not want to be named, such is the fear created by Crerar in the area, says that on the night of or, at the latest, the night following the disappearance of Deirdre Jacob she was awoken at about 3 a.m. by what she thought were the screams of a human in considerable pain.

> It seemed to go on for ages and then stopped. I was at the time a very heavy sleeper and it would take a lot to wake me. It was a horrible sound, like someone being tortured. I know the quarry well, having played there as a child and the screams were coming from the wooded section not far from my house. I am sure it was getting bright when I fell back asleep. I told myself that what I heard could have been the cries of an animal, but I am now convinced they were that of a human.

Sometime later, about a month, this witness and neighbours noticed a dreadful stench emanating from the direction of the quarry. People in the area are convinced that the quarry contains human remains and US experts on tracing missing persons claim that some serial killers dispose of bodies within a convenient radius of where they live so that they can easily satisfy their desire to return to the scene of the crime.

This evidence disturbs John McGuinness, Fianna Fáil TD for Carlow/Kilkenny, who has for years been fighting for justice for the Dullard family and those of the disappeared on the basis of what he says is a totally inadequate system for tracing missing persons in this country.

Certainly I believe that if John Crerar was seen the night after Jo Jo disappeared at the quarry of course it should be searched. It should have been checked out a long time ago. But this is typical of the inept way that the gardaí go about setting up an operation for a missing person. We are way behind other countries in this regard. Over the years, in the wake of Jo Jo's disappearance, with the support and co-operation of her sister Mary Phelan and the family I have done extensive research on the matter.

Earlier this year we travelled to the United States where we studied the latest models used there in the search for missing persons. We succeeded in getting offers of expertise and technology which would be donated free to the gardaí. As yet we have had no response. The methods employed here are completely inadequate.

This is the other side of the tragedy of those missing presumed dead – the nagging doubts that never go away, as well as the constant search for a resolution. Mary Phelan has campaigned for years, writing to politicians, getting posters and leaflets printed, petitioning signatures, all the mind-numbing and physically exhausting activities that go with trying to get things changed.

For Mary and many others, normal life went out the door after their loved ones disappeared. Nothing would ever be the same again except for the constant torment. 'A lot of families that I have spoken to over the years did not cope well,' says Mary. 'I know of two marriages that have broken up because of the strain, one relative who has developed diabetes and someone else who is receiving psychiatric treatment.'

Extracts from a diary kept by Mary Phelan supplies graphic evidence of the daily torment that families of the missing suffer. It is a chronicle of hope followed rapidly by despair, a tale of heartbreak, tears but above all a story of single-minded devotion to the memory of a loved one. It demonstrates the point that the serial killer does not just murder the victim but also consigns the relatives to a lifetime of misery. The family were reduced to such a pit of despair that when the decomposed body of a female was taken from the Shannon they prayed that it was Jo Jo's mortal remains.

1995

November 9   Jo Dullard disappeared at approximately 11.39 p.m.

November 10   Kathleen Bergin, my sister, rang myself at 7 p.m. to say that Jo Jo had not returned home and asked me if she was with me at Cuffsgrange. I told Kathleen to ring the gardaí, which would have been at approximately 8 p.m. Routine questions were asked.

November 11   Kathleen went to the gardaí at Callan at 3 p.m. to see if there was any news of Jo. At 10 p.m. CKR and KCR radio put out the news of Jo's disappearance.

November 12 The gardaí rang me to say they have no news of Jo.

November 13 Gardaí rang to ask me to come to Callan Barracks. Just routine questioning. All day news was out on nationwide radio stations of Jo's disappearance. It was out on *Crimeline* and all the national papers. We asked gardaí in Callan for the army.

November 14 I went to Callan Barracks at 11 a.m. The gardaí ask me to go on television to make an appeal to the public for information on Jo's disappearance.

November 15 Two detectives called to the house from Kilkenny barracks, Superintendent Vincent Duff and Detective Adrian Roche. They had no news of Jo.

November 17 Garda Harry O'Brien called to us from Callan Barracks. My brother Tom O'Reilly was here. Garda O'Brien proceeded to take statements from the two of us.

November 20 I was on CKR with Sue Nunne to make an appeal for Jo. An offer came from a member of the public to give £1,000 reward for information on Jo. Also I was on Co Clare Radio. Detective Pat Starr came out to see us. He had no news.

November 21 I went on the *Pat Kenny Show* for another appeal.

November 22   No news of Jo from gardaí. *The Sunday World* newspaper called to the house.

November 23   RTÉ came at 12 p.m. for me to make a plea for Jo.

November 27   Superintendent Vincent Duff called this morning to say that he had no news of Jo.

November 30   It was on the news that a girl had seen Jo getting into the back of a car the night she disappeared. On hearing this news we went to Kilkenny Barracks and spoke with Detective Jim Ryan regarding the news of Jo. He said he could not say much about it. That night Detective Roche rang and said they were looking into the girl's claim.

December 2   We went into Kilkenny Barracks and spoke with Garda William Powell. He had no news of Jo but said he would call out to us sometime.

December 4   I rang Michael Lally at RTÉ Waterford to ask for a plea to go back out on television. He said that if there were further developments he would put it out again.

December 6   We went to Kilkenny Barracks this afternoon. No news on Jo. No news had developed from the girl who saw Jo getting into the back of the car.

December 8   Kathleen Bergin, Mary Cullinane and myself went to Kilkenny Barracks at 1 p.m.

and spoke with Detective Jim Ryan. He showed us some clothes they had found. He asked us if they were Jo's. None belonged to Jo. Detective Ryan spoke about us going on *Crimeline*. Detective Brian Murphy drove us to RTÉ in Dublin. *Crimeline* was then filmed.

December 11 The reconstruction of Jo's disappearance went out on *Crimeline*.

December 13 Detective Jim Ryan rang. Could I bring personal belongings to the station for a clairvoyant. I could not get anything that day as I hadn't got any way of getting into Jo's flat. Kathleen Bergin, my sister, had the key.

December 14 Kathleen Bergin and myself went to Detective Ryan with some belongings of Jo's.

December 19 *The Daily Mirror* came to the house. I gave them photos of Jo.

December 21 I rang Superintendent Vincent Duff to put an appeal on television for Christmas. I also phoned Marty Whelan's TV programme. He put out an appeal for Jo. *The Irish Times* were here. They did a story on Jo for Christmas.

December 24 Kathleen came to my house with Jo's ring in response to Detective Ryan's request for the clairvoyant.

Christmas Day We left here at 2.45 p.m. We went to my parents' grave. Then we went to Milford Lock and then to Moone, searching. We came home at 8.30 p.m. I thought that, because it was Christmas Day, we might find Jo ourselves. That day was very cold and was a very sad time for us. We could not bring ourselves to eat Christmas lunch. We just had tea and toast. Jo's killer is having dinner with his family but poor Jo will never know Christmas again.

December 26 Detective Ryan came at 11 a.m. for Jo's ring. We then left for Moone. I took the phone number and just lifted the phone to see if I could get a feeling. We went into the church and lit a few candles and prayed for our dear Jo. We came home at 6 p.m. Detective Ryan wished us good news.

December 27 We went out again to Moone, searching.

This was the last entry for 1995. It goes on, unrelentingly focusing on the smallest of detail, hunting for a break and searching for a meaning that would give the smallest piece of sense to an experience that should not be visited on decent folk.

1996

January 1 Detective Ryan came back with Jo's ring.

	He was very caring and hoped that we got through the Christmas okay.

January 6 Detective Ryan came for a pair of jeans belonging to Jo.

January 8 We went to Labour TD Seamus Pattison to set up a meeting with Nora Owen [then Minister for Justice].

January 9 I left a schoolbook with the gardaí with Jo's handwriting at their request.

January 10 Went on local radio stations with appeal. Went to Seamus Pattison again and were told that we would see Nora Owen within a week.

January 11 Seamus Pattison rang. We will meet Nora Owen on January 15.

The meeting was subsequently cancelled and the diary goes on to detail meetings with media and investigators. Finally the meeting with Nora Owen was confirmed for January 22.

January 22 Left home at 5 a.m. Went to brother Tom in Kildare to drop off the children. We arrived at Department of Justice at 11 a.m. We spoke with Nora Owen and asked if she had any ideas to help us. She said she had a report from the gardaí and that everything was being done. We asked if the army could be brought in too. She replied: 'Where shall

I send them? We have no specific area.'

She then told us of a relation that had gone missing. He turned up a year later. I think that she was trying to make us think that Jo had just run away. She then said that Jo could be found come springtime as people would be out walking. She said if we wanted help again we could contact her office. We felt we came out of her office no wiser than when we went in.

January 25   Jo's twenty-second birthday. Still no news. We had a birthday Mass in Cuffsgrange.

The diary continues to record the detail of media contact and communication with the investigators and the constant appeals. There was a 999 call from a girl with information.

February 16   Detective Frank Byrne rang from Baltinglass to say that they had the 999 girl and she was in a car that gave Jo a lift. The 999 girl said that she had got out at the traffic lights in Carlow and that Jo had gone on with the two men. I rang Frank Byrne back. At around 7 p.m. he told me that the 999 girl might not lead us to Jo and not to get our hopes up.

February 19   Gardaí rang from Baltinglass to say that a conference in Carlow with gardaí was being held and I was asked not to make any appeals for the moment.

February 20   News had leaked out that the 999 girl had come forward.

March 3   Mass in Callan for Jo.

March 5   Went on KCR radio in Naas. I met a detective and told him that I had a dream of Jo, my mother, father and the faces of two men that I did not know. I said that I'd get an artist to draw the two faces and that might help with the investigation. He showed me all the folders of information and said that since I went on the *Pat Kenny Show* a lot of new information came in.

An artist subsequently made a representation of the faces in Mary's dream and Mary brought them to the investigation team. But whether this seemed like clutching at straws, hope is hope. However, a dream of the face of the killer is not enough to identify him, just more evidence of the torment he has caused.

March 14   Detective Harrington rang and said it's like day one, no news of Jo.

April 1   Went to see a private investigator and told him about Jo. He agreed to work for us.

April 28   Drove to Moone, went into the church and lit candles for Jo, went into the phone box. Someone had left a holy picture asking for a miracle to bring Jo back.

April 29 Rang Commissioner Byrne to make an appointment. He made an appointment for 3 p.m. May 3.

May 3 We took the 11.14 a.m. train to Dublin, arrived at the Garda Headquarters at 2.15 p.m. Met Commissioner Byrne at 2.40 p.m. We had a very successful meeting. I explained about the vision I had. The Commissioner was told about us requesting the army.

May 7 We had a Mass in the house. Father Campion came, as he knew of the vision and also of things happening in the house, which we had all experienced and we felt Jo's spirit was here. We had the Mass for her, in the hope she could rest.

On May 30 there was a meeting with Bertie Ahern whom the family agreed was very sympathetic. He said he would put it to Nora Owen that the army should search for Jo Jo. He said he could see no reason why the army should not be called out. Mary felt that they got a far better hearing than from Nora Owen.

June 26 I was very sad to hear of the news that Veronica Guerin had been murdered. This lady was killed fighting to make a better country for us to live in. I'm so sad at her terrible death. I had spoken with Veronica a few times and found her to be truly wonderful. We all sat here with the children, Imelda and Melvin, and said prayers for this brave woman. God bless her.

There were more and more references in the diary of the possibility of the army going out, but nothing was happening. Mary's frustration in the autumn of the year is evident from this entry.

Aug 9   Detective Jim Ryan and Detective Brian Murphy came out at my request and we told them just how upset we were. I could not help it but I broke down in tears. They were so very helpful. Detective Ryan said he would do his best to set up a meeting with the investigating team.

This edited diary is a powerful evocation of the grief that is suffered by relatives of a missing loved one, whose body has never been found and is presumed dead.

Mary Phelan with the help of John McGuinness TD has transferred her grief and frustration into an untiring campaign to better the lot of the relatives of missing people. They have now become so expert on the subject that even the introduction of Operation Trace did not impress them.

'I was not impressed with the speed of development [of

Operation Trace] or that it was the proper model for dealing with the problem,' says McGuinness. 'Operation Trace had exactly the same approach and information sharing as was there already.'

McGuinness may well be right but with the best will in the world and the latest computer technology, if there are no solid leads, clear suspects or bodies, the operation had no chance of success. On the other hand what John McGuinness, Mary Phelan and the relatives of other missing people want does not seem unreasonable, given the track record in regard to the missing and presumed dead women. What they want is:

1. A permanent Garda unit to specifically investigate missing persons.
2. The forty-eight hour time lapse between the filing of a missing persons report and the initiation of a Garda investigation to be replaced by a rapid response.
3. The provision of counselling for the next of kin.
4. A twenty-four hour helpline.
5. Financial assistance to help look for missing relatives.

But in December 2002 the campaign received a big setback when Commissioner Pat Byrne decided not to set up a special missing persons unit. Mary Phelan found the decision 'absolutely appalling'.

> We have been campaigning from day one. Police in the UK, US and Australia have such units. It was used in the Holly and Jessica case in Soham. We have nothing here. None of the families of the missing women are happy about how the gardaí investigated the cases.

John McGuinness TD found the decision 'deeply disappointing' and wanted to know if the commissioner would consider bringing in expertise from an outside force.

> I asked him to compare what was done by the gardaí and the operation carried out by British police in the Jessica and Holly case. It is incredible that the families of the missing had to go to America to find out FBI protocols for dealing with missing people and bring back knowledge the gardaí already knew.

Despite the despair suffered by the family Mary Phelan and her relatives have, through the years of campaigning, provided not only a fitting legacy to the memory of their dead sister but also great hope and comfort to the families of other missing people. The Jo Jo Dullard Memorial Trust was set up in 1998 by Mary and her husband Martin Phelan, with the help of John McGuinness TD.

16
MISSING PRESUMED DEAD

There has been a huge increase in violence and murder in Ireland and a veritable explosion of murders of women, many which have gone unsolved. There has also been a new addition to the canon of crime, gangland assassination, which largely goes unpunished. The increase is not the only disturbing factor. The nature of the murders and the methods to both carry out the crime and ensure that the murderers will not be apprehended are more savage and sophisticated.

Stretching back to 1979, the murders reached a climax in the nineties. The list of unsolved murders of women during this period is very worrying in regard to the nature of the killers and the inability of the gardaí to catch them. To be fair, when there is no direct connection between perpetrator and victim it makes the task more difficult but any night's viewing of the crime slot on the Discovery Channel reveals just how successful police counterparts in the US are at solving the most difficult instances of murders in this category.

To posit the theory that this success is linked to greater resources is spurious. Better expertise, undoubtedly but the vast geographical area and the ability of the killers to move quickly from State to State makes the task far more difficult than in a small country, particularly when a sizeable number of killings are confined to one small area in Ireland – Leinster.

A roll call of murders of women between 1979 and 1998 makes depressing reading not only because the killers of the missing have never been brought to justice but also because of the number of bodies that have never been found, causing lasting and unmerciful grief to the relatives of the victims.

The father of American Annie McCarrick, the first woman to disappear without trace, summed up the feelings of hopelessness and despair that the lack of resolution inflicts on the family.

> All the joy has been taken out of everything. You look to things to fill your day and you think that they are going to take your mind off it, but there are reminders every time your eyes blink of what you are missing.
>
> It's a walking death. There is no closure, no end and the only closure that I can think of is the one that I don't want. The big thing is that it doesn't go away.

The pain of these words have echoed in the hearts of eight other Irish families who have never been given the opportunity by the killers of their daughters and sisters to grieve. They will be haunted until they enter their own graves by the thoughts of what happened to their loved ones. One father could take it no more and ended his own life.

Postmortems on the bodies of those women who have been found, such as Phyllis Murphy, Marie Kilmartin and Antoinette Smith, show that the victims were savagely killed, raped and strangled by men who showed a wanton disregard for the suffering and terror they instilled in the victims, in other words, all the classical signs of the serial killer. One can only speculate about the exact fate of the disappeared women, but experts can make an educated guess from the pattern of abductions and it is more than likely that the missing women suffered similar deaths to those who were found.

Their killers, however, had learnt a valuable lesson: dispose of the body successfully and it is almost impossible to solve the crime. They know that without a crime scene or body they cannot be caught. They also have to be ultra careful of not being caught by chance, as many such killers are. The burial ground has to be within easy reach but in an inaccessible area. Mountain and bog areas, however remote, have in the past failed to adequately hide the bodies from discovery.

The list of dead and missing women looks like this:

1979   Phyllis Murphy (21) last seen December 22, 1979. Body found in January 1980. John Crerar convicted of the murder, November 2002.

1982   Patricia Furlong (21) strangled. Body found in a field near the Fraughan Festival. Vinnie Connell convicted of the murder in December 1991, his conviction later quashed by the Court of Criminal Appeal.

1987   Antoinette Smith (27), a separated mother of two, disappeared on July 12 from Dublin after attending a David Bowie concert in Slane. Body found at the Feather Beds, Glendoo, Killakee in the Dublin mountains in 1988 (unsolved).

1991   Patricia Doherty (30) left home in Tallaght on December 23 for last-minute shopping. Body found in a collapsed peat bank near Killakee in the Dublin mountains in June 1992 (unsolved).

1992 Grace Livingstone, a middle-aged woman, found dead in her home in north County Dublin. She had been tied up and shot in the head (unsolved).

1993 Annie McCarrick (26), US citizen working in Dublin, last seen in Johnny Fox's pub in the Dublin mountains, March 26 (body never found).

Marie Kilmartin (36) disappeared December 16 from Portlaoise, body found in June 1994 in bog at Pims Road off the Mountmellick to Portlaoise Road (unsolved).

1994 Eva Brennan (40) disappeared after leaving her parents' home in Rathgar on July 23 (body never found).

Imelda Keenan (22) last seen in Waterford City, January 3 (body never found).

1995 Josephine 'Jo, Jo' Dullard (20) Callan. Last heard at 11.30 p.m. from a phone kiosk at Moone, Co Kildare, November 9 (body never found).

Marilyn Rynn, last seen December 23, Dublin City centre. Body found two weeks later near home in Blanchardstown. David Lawler convicted of murder (semen of the killer preserved by sub-zero winter temperatures).

1996 Veronica Guerin (36) *Sunday Independent* journalist assassinated by members of drugs gang June 26, 1996. Paul Ward convicted of the murder, cleared on appeal, Brian Meehan convicted of the murder. Is appealing. John Gilligan charged with the murder. Prosecution failed.

Fiona Pender (25), seven months pregnant, last seen leaving flat in Church Street, Tullamore, August 23 (body never found).

Sophie Toscan Du Plantier (39) murdered savagely with over forty wounds to her body December 23 in West Cork (unsolved).

Belinda Pereira, Sri Lankan prostitute, beaten to death in an apartment in Liffey Street, Dublin, December 29 (unsolved).

1997 Eileen O Shaughnessey (48), Galway taxi driver, found bludgeoned to death in a country laneway outside Galway city on December 1, 1997 (unsolved).

Ciara Breen (17) last seen leaving home in Dundalk on February 13. She took no possessions with her (body never found).

Mary Callinan and Sylvia Shields died March 9 after a monstrous knife attack with pyscho-sexual overtones in Grangegorman, Dublin (unsolved).

Catherine Doyle and her husband Carl died August 15 after a savage knife attack at their home in Roscommon. Mark Nash convicted.

1998 Fiona Sinnott (19) last seen in a house in Wexford on February 9 (body never found).

Deirdre Jacob (19) last seen walking along the Brennanstown Road, Newbridge, Co Kildare on July 28 (body never found).

1999 September 3 Raonaid Murray (17) savagely murdered near her home in Dun Laoghaire, Co Dublin (unsolved).

2002   April 2 Catherine Byrne (21) body found in a flat in South
Circular Road, Dublin owned by Joseph Burke also found
dead at the scene (unsolved).

This list does not include the many murders of women in other
situations, categorised as domestic or relationship, by husbands,
partners or, increasingly, by depressed men killing their families. It
also excludes drink- or drug-fuelled violence. It makes for
frightening and depressing evidence of the ever-present threat to
Irish women of violence, rape and murder from men of increasingly
psychotic leaning.

Life has become cheap here. Both statistics and experience of
violence give us this message. Dead men come cheaply but, as
always, the women are cheaper and more vulnerable. From 1992 on
there have been thirty-five unsolved murders of men. A sizeable
portion were accounted for by gangland activities including
contract killings, drug turf wars and internecine feuds. There were
few innocents involved with the exception of some victims of
violent robbery. The women were innocent citizens going about the
ordinary business of life.

And it is safe to deduce that the killers of innocent women were
also men with even more twisted, base and perverted minds than
the criminal hit men who, in most cases, simply gunned down their
quarries. To understand why this should be so, it is important to go
beyond the statistics and attempt to grapple with the degeneration
of Irish society. These monsters are not simply created overnight.
They are aided and abetted by the breakdown of law and order, the
family unit and the basic values of the country as a whole.

One of the few journalists in the past years, apart from Veronica Guerin, to analyse this horrible phenomenon is Geraldine Niland who, in the wake of Veronica's death, wrote extensively on the sort of murders we are dealing with in this book. Niland has developed an expertise in the whole area of psychotic and serial killing in this country.

An article she wrote for *The Sunday Independent* published on January 28, 2001, is particularly instructive on the subject of how and why the demography of murder has changed so radically in this country.

In the article Niland deals with the subject with the help of criminologist Paul O'Mahoney who says that the ready resort to lethal violence by criminals, and the presence of a number who are prepared to kill in cold blood for pay or under instructions, marks an unwelcome development in Irish crime. He says that public concern about this new level of brutality is entirely justified. The vast majority of such killers and those who control them go undetected.

He points to the amalgamation of the two separate worlds of city and rural life, the development of the criminal infrastructure and the increased drugs trade as factors which make Ireland like all other Western countries. He believes that the far-reaching social changes of the past three decades are part of the country's metamorphosis from the traditional agricultural society into a largely consumer population composed of far more isolated nuclear families.

As everything becomes more developed, so do the forms of killing. For example, crime-related assassinations are at the root of the big boost in homicides. The emergence of sex crimes is another worrying development.

Life in provincial centres like Cork, Limerick and Sligo is not that much different from that in Dublin.

There has been a huge increase in violence and murder in Cork and Limerick. The latter always had a reputation for random knife attacks and killings that earned it the sobriquet 'Stab City'. But the knives have been replaced with an array of guns, including highly sophisticated weapons which are now used to settle feuds and create a spate of murders, most recently centred around the bloody battle between the Keane and Ryan families.

Our self-image, the criminologist maintains, must expand to take in the more horrendous aspects of our behaviour – rape, assassination, child abuse by family and clergy, killing and rape of the elderly, the murder of four children as part of two different suicides by parents, and growing random violence. He believes that the rising levels of rape and sexual assaults as well as murder of women and the increase in domestic violence underlines the insidious nature and pervasive influence of violence in Irish society.

It is against the background of these unwelcome changes in Irish criminal behaviour that those eight women disappeared without trace. Despite individual Garda investigations and the setting up of a specific unit, Operation Trace, the fate of those missing women remains a mystery today. So what has happened to them? Can we speculate with any degree of accuracy and what is the specific effect of those disappearances?

Geraldine Niland has pored over the mystery and attempted to answer these questions for many years.

> Operation Trace has now been phased out without any breakthrough in the cases. While technically all these women remain missing persons, it is now likely that most of them have been murdered in as yet undetermined circumstances. In all these cases, the desperate pain suffered by the families of these lost daughters and sisters cannot be over-stressed as the years pass by.
>
> While investigations by Operation Trace have found no links to one prime suspect, the haunting spectre of a multiple killer persists. In this context also, the emergence of the persistent trend of unsolved murders of women is a fact that cannot be set aside. The possibility of the killer or killers re-offending has become an unknown quantity which places the lives of women at risk.

Operation Trace focused on six of the disappearances which fell within a geographical area concentrated mainly in the east Leinster area. The six cases were then divided into separate categories of three by the emergence of individual circumstances in the cases. The cases were Annie McCarrick, March 1993, Jo Jo Dullard, November 1995, Fiona Pender, August 1996; Ciara Breen, February 1997; Fiona Sinnott, February 1998, Deirdre Jacob, July 1998.

The cases of Annie McCarrick, Jo Jo Dullard and Deirdre Jacob were considered separately because of the circumstances of the disappearances, the fact that they occurred within a small radius (the first in Wicklow and the second two in Kildare), and the timescale involved. The disappearances were punctuated by intervals of thirty-two months.

By coincidence, or perhaps not, within the even smaller radius of Kildare is Colgan's Cut where Phyllis Murphy was raped and murdered and her case solved by the very investigation team looking into the disappearances of these women many years later.

It may also be a coincidence but these three young women have similar dark hair and innocent, wide-eyed faces of unspoilt good looks. Male killers, no more than ordinary men, have a propensity to hunt women with a certain preferred look.

The other three women, Fiona Pender, Fiona Sinnott and Ciara Breen, are accepted by both investigators and journalists such as Geraldine Niland and Barry Cummins, who dealt with the disappeared in his book *Missing*, as cases which have prime suspects connected in some way to the victims. This rules out those killers of the random or rehearsed psycho killer category. Whoever killed those women and, in one case, an unborn child had, however appalling, a reason, individually connected to the victim, to carry out the crime.

In all cases the perpetrators have successfully disposed of the bodies. Regardless of intent or premeditation, connection or no, the killers have displayed a cool efficiency. The bodies, simply and starkly, have never been found.

American student Annie McCarrick (26) vanished during a trip to the Dublin mountains and, despite a massive Garda search, no clues were found. She left her flat in Sandymount in the early afternoon of Friday March 26, 1993. She first caught a number 18 bus to Ranelagh and sometime around 4 p.m. she got on a 44 bus heading for Enniskerry Village. Earlier in the day she had asked a friend to accompany her but the friend was indisposed and so Annie decided to go on her own. This also suggested that she had made no arrangement to meet anyone at her destination, whatever that was.

Anyone who knows the environs of Enniskerry and Powerscourt is familiar with the beautiful scenery but which can also be treacherous. Powerscourt Waterfall has claimed many victims falling from the summit. The woods surrounding the demesne are wild and scattered but usually well traversed, especially at the weekends. Nonetheless the woods, which cover many an incline, gorge and isolated copse, are not recommended to be negotiated alone, for any number of reasons based on health and safety. Certainly not by a woman travelling alone. That is, if the estate and the woods was Annie's destination.

There was a positive sighting of Annie by an ex-work colleague on the 44 bus. There was no sighting of the attractive and distinctively attired American woman in the village itself, where the bus terminus is, or on the road to Powerscourt.

After a public appeal, a doorman at Johnny Fox's pub in Glencullen, which lies four miles from Enniskerry, contacted the gardaí to say that he recognised the woman on the posters as one who was in the pub on the night that Annie disappeared. Another doorman confirmed this, saying he saw her in the back lounge at about 9.30 p.m. The first doorman said that the woman was in the company of a young man who had paid the cover charge for them both into the lounge where music was being played.

If this was indeed Annie the obvious question is how did she get there – on foot, was she offered a lift in a car or had she arranged to meet someone? She was due in work in Café Java in Leeson Street the following morning and had invited friends over for dinner in her apartment in Sandymount in the evening. It was hardly likely that she was going out for a late night in Johnny Fox's pub, so far away from both work and home.

Nor indeed is there any explanation why Annie, given the commitments she had the following day, would take two buses to a relatively remote destination in the late afternoon at a time of year when dusk would fall early, giving her little time to indulge her love of walking and the Irish countryside. It would have been almost 5 p.m. by the time the bus arrived in Enniskerry. Too many questions and no answers. It was not as if the victim, of what gardaí treated from the beginning as a murder investigation, was anything but an organised and utterly reliable person.

Nothing about this case makes any sense to anyone except to the perpetrator of the crime who, either opportunistically or to a rehearsed plan, given the opportunity, decided to indulge his psychotic tendencies. Those tendencies have long been studied and are now well known to include rape, strangulation and burial, and the conscious and brutal defiling of the female form. Tendencies that do not go away but are inflamed and perpetuated by the perceived success of getting away with murder.

The search operation mounted in the wake of Annie McCarrick's disappearance was one of the biggest in the history of missing persons investigations. In the first year 400 people were interviewed and statements were taken from 200 and yet the details of what happened were no further enhanced by this large and laborious gathering of information. The victim vanished without a trace.

One year after her disappearance, Annie McCarrick's father John, a former police officer, came over from New York and offered a $150,000 reward for information. Not even the size of the reward elicited one more iota of knowledge. That a massive hunt of such scale should produce only one sighting on a bus and another in a pub, which could not be accepted as totally reliable, beggars belief.

The case had all the feeling of a one-off, something out of the ordinary that could not possibly happen again. Most journalists and investigators believed that to be the case. They would never have believed how wrong they would be and that it would happen again and again with disturbing regularity.

Jo Jo Dullard and Deirdre Jacob we will deal with in more detail in the next chapters. This does not diminish the importance of the other disappearances, they simply have other implications.

Fiona Pender's mother, Josephine, last saw her twenty-five-year-old daughter on Friday August 23, 1996 at the young woman's flat in Church Street, Tullamore. The women had been shopping for the baby that Fiona was expecting.

Fiona's boyfriend, John Thompson, said that he last saw her at 6 a.m. the same morning before he went to work. The couple were hoping to get a house and he was working long hours on his father's farm. Fiona's mother called to the flat later that evening but it was in darkness. She thought her daughter had gone out with friends who were over from America.

The following day, Saturday, after evening Mass Josephine called again but there was still no answer. She was worried and after returning home, phoned John at his father's farm. He said he thought Fiona was staying at her mother's. He came home immediately and he and Josephine went into the flat. There was no sign of disturbance. They then went to the local police station and reported Fiona missing. But from the Garda perspective, she was an adult and there was no evidence of a struggle or that she had been abducted against her will.

It was the following day that a full missing persons operation was put in place. Clearly valuable time had been lost. Whoever had been involved in Fiona's disappearance would have had the time to murder her and dispose of her body without any public awareness that a young woman was missing.

The flat and its contents were examined closely, but revealed nothing of any evidential value. There was nothing to indicate where Fiona had gone or with whom she had left the flat. In the following weeks waterways and lands were searched without success.

Investigators believe there was a motive for her murder, which for legal reasons cannot be examined in this book. A person who might have had a motive has been questioned by gardaí who believe that the victim's body is buried in the Slieve Bloom mountains. The nature of the terrain, like the Dublin mountains, offers hiding places that may never be found or provide any connection with the killer.

There were the inevitable sightings of Fiona, each lead exhaustively followed. In the absence of a confession or the body, the abduction and murder of Fiona Pender will remain a cold case.

Fiona's brother Mark had pre-deceased her in June 1995 and as a result of the stress of her disappearance her father, Sean, took his own life on March 31, 2000. The abductor of his daughter is responsible for three deaths, a young woman, an unborn child and a father who could not bear the pain any longer.

Ciara Breen (17) of Bachelor's Walk, Drogheda, Co Louth, vanished in the middle of the night on February 13, 1997. The teenager who lived with her mother, Bernadette, worked at Ógra Dún Dealgan, an early school-leaver's employment project. Both mother and daughter had a meal in the Roma Restaurant, Park Street, Dundalk on the night in question and returned home around 10 p.m. Ciara told her mother that she was going to bed.

Sometime later in the night Bernadette looked into Ciara's room but she was not there. The window was open indicating that her daughter had slipped out. She had taken no clothes or possessions with her so it was clear that she intended to return home. But she never did and has not been seen since. At the time she was also having complicated dental work carried out on her front teeth, another reason that she would not have left voluntarily.

Investigators believe that she was going to meet a man with whom she had become friendly. There is a man who is suspected to have been involved in Ciara's disappearance but there is not sufficient evidence to bring him to trial.

One year later Fiona Sinnott (19) went missing after being seen by her former boyfriend, the father of her baby daughter, at her isolated rented house at Ballyhitt, four miles outside Rosslare, Co Wexford, on the morning of February 9, 1998. She had been socialising in a nearby pub the night before but, because she had been complaining of pain in her arm, her former partner had accompanied her home and slept the night on the sofa. She had intended to go to a doctor later that morning and he gave her money before being collected from the house by his mother.

Nothing has ever been heard of the teenager since. Again, investigators believe that she knew the man who was responsible for her disappearance, and, again, any further investigation is hampered by the absence of the young girl's body.

Fiona Sinnott had led a rather chequered career in terms of relationships. She had been previously subjected to a number of assaults by a former boyfriend, which ended in hospital treatment. But in the fashion typical of many women beaten by their husbands or boyfriends she had never made an official complaint to the gardaí. Unless she named the perpetrator of this abuse, there was nothing that the authorities could do, nor could they form a consistent pattern to point to the man responsible for her disappearance. Suspicion without corroboration is no proof. And the gardaí had plenty of suspicions, provided in part by her abject experiences, which included at least once being at the hands of one man who had beaten her to a pulp.

In the wake of her disappearance gardaí followed up every lead that came their way and brought in a number of people for questioning. In a rural area rumour is followed by counter-rumour and people can point the finger of suspicion for entirely personal and selfish reasons. But good police know that, however tenuous the information seems to be, it has to be pursued until it is found wanting beyond all doubt. In Fiona Sinnott's case every avenue led to a cul de sac.

What is extraordinary about these, the missing, is how efficiently they were spirited away, with not a clue left behind to establish who, how and ultimately where they were taken. If we are to accept that there seems to be absolutely no link whatsoever between the last mentioned cases, then it is quite extraordinary how the three men involved acquired the considerable expertise to be able to get rid of the bodies without leaving any trace.

It is not an easy task to get rid of a body that might by sheer chance surface or be spotted by the casual walker or hunter. Even Shaw and Evans carefully weighting the bodies of their victims could never have predicted that the sea would deliver the body of Elizabeth Plunkett as Lake Inagh might have the body of Mary Duffy had they not confessed. If the professionals fail, how come the amateurs succeed? It makes one wonder.

17
WRONG PLACE, WRONG TIME?

The grief of the relatives of the disappeared is intensified like the ordinarily bereaved by the constant flood of memory and the tide of flashback. Unlike the bereaved there is no healing offered by the passage of time. The incidents and things that pass most of us by are given added significance in the awful battle to achieve some understanding of what has happened: what the person was wearing at the time and what was left behind in the living space they had occupied.

A loved one cannot be mourned without a funeral, or buried without a body. The walking death, the lack of closure the constant and unrelenting search for the truth which some other human being has hidden as effectively as the body of the young girl that he, either alone or in concert with another, has buried. Destroying not only the evidence but peace forever for the victim's relatives. Some families are visited with far more than their fair share of grief in this valley of tears. The Dullard family of Callan, Co Kilkenny is certainly one, just like the Doyle family in Dublin and the Pender family of Tullamore and all the others. Each individual case has dreadful suffering which expands, like the effect of the stone thrown into the pond.

Jo Jo Dullard was a country girl, twenty-one years of age with a pragmatic and simple outlook on life, vivacious, good humoured and industrious. She was the youngest of a family of four from the village of Newtown who never knew her father who died a few months before she was born. Her mother died of cancer when she was ten years of age and she was brought up by her older sisters Kathleen and Mary.

After attending secondary school in the Convent of Mercy, Callan, Jo Jo spent a short period on work experience in the local newspaper *The Kilkenny People*. At nineteen she went to Dublin to do a course in beauty treatment but dropped out and ended up working in bars in the city, including the Red Parrot in Drumcondra. She shared a flat in Harold's Cross with a number of girlfriends including her closest friend Mary Cullinane.

Her sisters were worried about her living in Dublin which in the early-to-mid-nineties was developing a reputation as an increasingly violent environment, with gangland wars and murders an almost weekly occurrence. Ironically, not far from where she lived, a lock-up in the Greenmount Industrial Estate was the headquarters for the biggest drugs operation in the history of the State.

As it happened it was Jo Jo's ambition to return home. Life for a country girl of her personality in an unforgiving metropolitan atmosphere was not attractive and when she was offered a part-time job in a restaurant in Callan she jumped at it.

She got a small flat above a butcher's shop next to the restaurant but had to travel weekly to Dublin to sign on and collect her welfare cheque which she was still entitled to because of the restricted hours she was working. She was extremely happy at home now and at weekends she went dancing in Kilkenny city. In many ways, her sisters had nothing to worry about, because Josephine, or Jo Jo, was not only a very trustworthy person but open as well.

Jo Jo was clearly relishing her new-found independence and this was enhanced in early November 1995 when she was offered a full-time job at a local restaurant. She still hankered after the career of beautician and dreamed of running her own business. But things were going very well for her – she had a full-time job and her own place. And time on her side; given her sensible and hard-working nature it is more than likely that Jo Jo would have realised that dream of having her own business in her native town.

The full-time job meant that she would have to sign off the dole and on the morning of Thursday November 9, she travelled to Dublin by bus. She went to Harold's Cross post office where she collected her last entitlements of over €130 in cash. She then travelled into the city centre, where she met some friends for farewell drinks in Bruxelles pub off Grafton Street. She was having a good time and missed the 9.30 p.m. bus to Callan.

She had plenty of places to stay but, since she was due to start her shift at the restaurant at 9 a.m. the following morning, she caught the 10 p.m. commuter bus to Naas. From there she decided to hitch the rest of the journey. She was picked up and dropped off at Kilcullen at 11 p.m. It was a typical misty, dark November night. She got a second lift to the tiny village of Moone, Co Kildare, from a man bound for Baltinglass.

At 11.20 p.m. she phoned her friend Mary Cullinane to say she was stranded in, as she put it jokingly, of all places, Moone. Her friend urged her to book into a bed and breakfast, but Jo Jo said there was none around. She appeared to be in great form. While she was talking she was keeping an eye on the road for a car. The night was forbidding. It was late and she was still fifty miles from her destination.

She cut short the conversation when the headlights of a car illuminated the telephone box. She put out her thumb but the car did not stop. She had just resumed her conversation when another set of headlights came into view. She opened the door and hailed down the car. It stopped. Hurriedly she told Mary, 'I've got a lift.'

The receiver was put back in place. All that Mary was left with was the sound of the tone and then silence. She had no idea at the time that it would be a silence that would last forever. Jo Jo Dullard disappeared into the November night and not a trace of her has ever been found since.

Around 4 a.m. the phone rang in Mary Cullinane's house. It was a wrong number.

Two cars passed the isolated telephone box in Moone that night. One continued on and the other stopped. Had the first car stopped, everything might have turned out differently. But that is another of the great 'what ifs' that have tortured the minds of the family in the eight years that have passed since the receiver was put down.

Was Jo Jo Dullard in the wrong place at the wrong time?

The confirmed accounts of her movements that day show that they were entirely unpredictable, particularly later in the evening when she missed her bus back to Callan. The rest may be entirely in the realm of chance but stalkers are also roamers, like the fox waiting patiently for the opportunity. Given the opportunity, they are well prepared for the eventuality.

Also it is a truism that the victim's movements, life and behaviour become an open book while the perpetrator remains elusive and, unless apprehended, not given to close scrutiny. This is a mistake, according to the findings of the staff of Quantico and the experience of many law enforcement agencies in both the US and Britain. Unless the victim is engaged in dangerous activity such as prostitution or had direct contact with the possible killer, then close examination of their personalities, activities or background is of little consequence.

In the weeks succeeding the vanishing, a Garda investigation was mounted. The media got involved and the family gave a host of interviews in the hope that some word would spark someone's memory of one small clue that might explain what really happened that dark night in November of 1995.

While the investigators applied their expertise and volunteers searched the roads and poked in bushes and ditches searching for the tiniest of clues, the requisite nutter got involved as well as the usual production of a number of red herrings.

One which was considered by the family to be a serious breach of confidence was that three weeks before her disappearance Jo Jo travelled to England to have an abortion. This was true and given to the investigation team in the spirit that every small piece of information is of some consequence. Unfortunately it made its way into the press and the spin was that Jo Jo might have been depressed as a result. However it had absolutely nothing to do with the abduction and only added to the distress of the family.

A letter in an illegible scrawl was sent to a Carlow radio station from a person claiming to have murdered Jo Jo.

> I murdered the girl on Saturday night at 8 p.m.
> You will find her body at the bottom of the Royal
> Canal at Lucan. I am going to shoot myself now.

Some under-achieving people of unsound mind want some form of spurious recognition. But their missives only have the effect of wasting the time of the investigating team and of deflecting attention from the identity of the more credible suspects.

In another letter the writer claimed to have seen Jo Jo hitching at Castledermot, some miles on from Moone. Both the letter and sighting were discounted by the investigating team. It was the first of many new 'leads' that proved to be unfounded. The upshot of it all was nothing more than the bare fact that on that night a girl disappeared and was never seen again. As stark and simple and as disturbing as that.

Frustration breeds tension and, naturally enough, divisions appeared over time between the relatives and the authorities responsible for carrying out the search and investigation. Jo Jo's sisters Mary Phelan and Kathleen Bergin began a campaign, as a result of their experience, to draw attention to the inadequate methods that the State and the Garda authorities employ in tracking down the missing.

To say that they were inadequate, at the time, would be an understatement. But this specific area was just one of many in a larger picture where crime, violence, drug running and murder was the order of the day. Added to this, the State had starved crime fighters of resources. In other words, the criminals were running amok without any restraint to their actions or operations.

It has been pointed out that, a short distance from where Jo Jo lived in Harold's Cross, the biggest drugs racket in this country, taking in hundreds of millions in profits, was operating with impunity, as were gangland assassins all over the city. Clearly then if resources were absent at a level which presented a real threat to society, they would be entirely absent in the matter of a missing woman.

This fact would not go unnoticed by the men responsible for the abduction of the women. Like the drug runners, all they needed was a plan in place to dispose of the human goods so that they could continue to operate without fear of apprehension. The atmosphere and conditions were perfect for the psychotic killer. All the more so because even with the limited resources the investigation of these crimes – entirely new to the murder landscape – were being handled in a traditional and conventional manner.

Not once in the investigation, which wasted a lot of time following false leads, was there any reference to the type of man who might be responsible for this crime: his mentality, modus operandi, age, profile, employment, whether he was local or from outside the county, or how he might be recognised by his behaviour and activities. In other words the focus was on the victim instead of the perpetrator. In this case there was no body and therefore there was nothing to be gained by concentrating on the victim other than tracing her movements, which after a while have simple but limited value. The profile of a man who would pick up a young woman at random, then abduct, rape and strangle her, bury her body and destroy her clothes could tell a lot more about the crime.

The victim is an open book, but the killer a mystery until the text of his mind is prized open.

It is perhaps, natural to respond to such awful events in the canon of human cruelty by saying that the victim was in the wrong place at the wrong time. But in a sense that shifts the attention away from the perpetrator and towards the victim, as if there was something amiss by being in the situation, in the first instance.

But it can be argued that chance had absolutely nothing to do with the disappearance of any of the women, not least Jo Jo Dullard and another tragic victim who was abducted within a short distance of her own home, Deirdre Jacob.

Another extraordinary aspect in the cases of the missing women, presumed dead, is that there was not one sighting of Annie Mc Carrick, Jo Jo Dullard, Fiona Sinnott, Fiona Pender or Ciara Breen meeting anyone or being brought anywhere prior to their abduction. And this seems to be a common thread in all the cases of abduction and murder of women, even when the bodies have been found. With one notable exception.

The disappearance of Deirdre Jacob stands out as most extraordinary for two major reasons. One was the circumstances under which she disappeared and the second, the fact that her abduction was the last (known to date) of the series which had begun with the abduction of Annie McCarrick in 1993.

18
GONE IN BROAD DAYLIGHT

It was a beautiful summer's day at the end of July 1998. The town of Newbridge, Co Kildare was basking not only in the sunshine but in the reflected glory of the county GAA football team, which had taken the Senior Leinster Championship title for the first time in forty-two years, just two days before at Croke Park.

It was a time to be happy with the summer sunshine warming the youthful expectations of life. On Tuesday July 28 an eighteen-year-old student, home from a teacher-training course in England, was in just such a mood as she walked around Newbridge town doing some everyday chores. Deirdre Jacob had spent the weekend with some friends in Carrickmacross, Co Monaghan and was in the best of form.

Deirdre was a beautiful looking young woman with glistening jet-black hair and lovely big grey-green eyes set against a perfect oval face. Her boyfriend was coming over from England to visit her later in the summer. She had the whole world at her feet.

That day she had walked the short distance from her home in Roseberry to the town centre to help her grandmother in her shop at lunchtime. At 2.20 p.m. she went to the AIB bank on the main street to get a bank draft to pay her second year's fees at Strawberry Hill training college in London. There is a frame of her recorded on the closed-circuit security system. She then went to the post office to send off the draft. On the way she bumped into a number of people she knew. She spoke briefly to a friend at the pedestrian crossing and then began the mile walk back to her home at Roseberry.

The Barretstown road along which she walked passes Newbridge College and then narrows into a tree-lined laneway running alongside the Liffey. It would normally be busy with traffic moving from town to countryside or vice versa. Deirdre was last seen about 300 yards from her home at around 3 p.m. She never made it. Another young woman had vanished into thin air, this time in broad daylight within shouting distance of her destination.

It was the bright sunlight, the laneway open to traffic in either direction, the good conditions for possible witnesses that gave this abduction its special and in ways most shocking characteristic. Whoever was responsible for the disappearance of Deirdre Jacob took a risk that none of the other abductors had taken – the possibility of being seen, being identified and being caught. There was only one other comparison to this case and only one other man that would have taken such a risk.

Not even the desperate and depraved compulsion of Shaw and Evans would have led them to take such a risk. The one time that they picked up a woman hitchhiking in daylight, they let her out when she asked to go to the toilet as they approached a pub. They had always operated under the cover of darkness and they knew that to try it in broad daylight could blow their cover instantly.

But there was a depressing familiarity about the days and weeks that followed this, the last disappearance of a woman presumed dead. There was nothing found to indicate a struggle at the scene or anywhere further along the route. Appeals for information yielded little or nothing. The following headline appeared in *The Irish Times* of August 5, just over a week after Deirdre vanished, and summed up the mood.

GARDAÍ 'BAFFLED' BY DISAPPEARANCE
OF STUDENT TEACHER

The usual search operation was mounted and neighbours and friends joined Civil Defence teams, the Garda subaqua unit and sniffer-dog teams in the hunt for clues into the disappearance. But intensive combing of an area covering a three and a half mile radius of the house failed to uncover any clues.

In Newbridge posters relating to the disappearance provided a depressing contrast to the banner welcoming home the victorious Kildare football team. A friend of Deirdre's, with the same bob haircut and dressed in the same clothes – navy jeans, white Nike runners, a navy sweatshirt with the Nike logo on the front and a black shoulder bag with a Cat logo – took part in a reconstruction of Deirdre's last walk from the town to near her home.

Deirdre's parents, Michael and Bernadette, private people by nature had, like many other families of the missing, come into the limelight to make pleas for information and help. They had also to suffer the same frustrations as investigators when subjected to false leads and a hoax caller.

A man made three calls to the *Leinster Leader* claiming to have given Deirdre a lift in Carrickmacross the evening that she disappeared. He later sent a letter to her parents without giving his name but leaving certain clues to his identity. At the time detectives believed him to be genuine and the hopes of the parents were raised and they appealed for the man to establish direct contact. 'I definitely gave a girl matching that description a lift. I gave her a lift on the Clane to Maynooth Road and I left her in Carrickmacross,' the man said in taped message. He also claimed that the student teacher was trying to get away from a man in England who was giving her a hard time. This so-called lead naturally produced a frenzy of media activity and publicity. But not for the first time such unwarranted interference in an investigation raised hopes which would be cruelly dashed, and wasted valuable Garda time.

In time the man was interviewed by gardaí and admitted that he had lost a daughter in a tragic accident and only wanted to sympathise with the Jacob family. What he actually did was to raise their hopes, put them through misery and then dash all those hopes. He also cost the investigation a huge amount of wasted time, all the while deflecting attention from the possible identity of the abductor.

Just like the Jo Jo Dullard case, it was another cruel red herring which only deepened the nightmare that the girl's parents had been plunged into, day after day waiting for the phone call that might end their agony. But they knew in their hearts that their daughter would never have gone missing of her own volition and her dormant bank account seemed to confirm this.

So the months and then the years passed. Another young woman had vanished, another life had been wasted, another family devastated and another killer had got away with murder. The big question that occupied both the public and the authorities was when was the next abduction and murder going to take place?

It did not take a rocket scientist to work out that a pattern of abduction and killing had emerged and in a very small region of the country. Given there was a pattern and, in the case of three of the women, a constant period of time, thirty-two months, separating them, then it would only be a matter of time until the killer or killers struck again.

But the fact is that, after that fateful day in Roseberry, Deirdre Jacob proved to be the last woman to disappear. There was one more planned abduction but it went seriously wrong, by pure chance, and the perpetrator was caught. After that there were no more abductions and no more disappearances. According to experts this could not be explained by coincidence. So great is the compulsion of the lust killer that he just cannot stop unless he dies or is incarcerated in an asylum or prison. As one expert says:

> Everything about our studies, interviews with and experience of such men, tells us that they do not stop raping and killing until they are caught. They may leave certain intervals between the killings until the compulsion overtakes them and they strike again. In the history of psychotic and serial killing it is unknown for the participants to cease killing voluntarily.

After the imprisonment of two men, John Crerar and Larry Murphy, who lived within a short geographical distance of where three of the women disappeared, the pattern, which had been established with the abduction and probable murder of Annie McCarrick in 1993, ceased.

On the day before Deirdre Jacob vanished a carpenter by the name of Larry Murphy was working in Roseberry. Less than two years later, the apparently respectable married man with two children carried out a crime that had all the hallmarks of a sexual psychopath and serial killer. There is little doubt in experts' minds that Deirdre Jacob's movements had been monitored for a time in the days leading up to her disappearance and that she had been stalked on the day. And the behaviour of Murphy in carrying out his crimes, as well as his presence in Roseberry, makes him a prime suspect for the abduction of the eighteen-year-old.

Murphy was a freelance carpenter who moved around a lot from job to job, giving him a perfect cover for the surveillance of young women. He also had a disturbing track record. Once while driving a friend of his wife to her home when he was living in Castledermot, Co Kildare he suddenly veered off the road and stopped a distance down a boreen. There he molested her before he suddenly put his hands around her neck and began to throttle her. She managed to push him away, get out of the car and run. He followed her and begged her not to tell his wife. In the classical manner of many lust or serial killers, he had difficulties in relating to women and to mixing with them socially in a normal manner. This translated into resentment and anger towards females and a desire to control them by violent means. Murphy expressed his own personal inadequacy by staring at women in pubs until they felt uncomfortable and looked away.

If this was the only relief for his hang up, he might have been considered a bit of an odd ball, a man who portrayed a macho characteristic by aggressively staring down his female foe and getting off on a feeling of power. But such behaviour in his type is just the curtain behind which lurks much more devious and dangerous inclinations. Murphy, just like Mark Nash, probably lived out a secret fantasy role and in his neck of the woods more akin to the Wild West, a cowboy hunting down his quarry, fearless and to be feared. The Man With No Name as opposed to the gun-toting hood, Vincent Vega.

He had another pastime, which, innocent for most, gave another clue to this type of pysche. He had a legally held weapon, a shotgun, and he would go hunting alone in the remote woods of the Wicklow mountains, a perfect stomping ground for the playing out of his fantasies. A grim but useful rehearsal, using animals instead of women. Either way he cast himself in the role of the Hunter, which also requires another skill – that of stalking. A poor stalker makes for a bad hunter. Tracking down is the very essence of the activity.

Under the cover of nature Murphy proved to be an excellent hunter, in direct contrast to his poor performance in the open social milieu of the pub. His crudeness in the latter situation conferred an image of a fool trying his imagined charm on and failing miserably. This would not help his damaged self-esteem, rather enhance his sense of failure. Once, in a pub, his crudeness over-spilled and he tried to grope a woman who was passing. It was an action, characteristic of his social ineptitude, that he would live to regret.

Perhaps, like Nash, he heard the laughter and the mocking of those who looked on. Men like these cannot tolerate the smallest humiliation. In his mind there would be an even greater need for revenge and control, carried out best in the territory where he knew he held sway – in the forest. But women do not wander the woods alone, he would have to get them on the street or even in the town.

A man who would risk his marriage and his future by attacking a family friend will stop at nothing to ensnare a stranger. Larry Murphy was such a man one night in the depths of winter, in February 2000. He was stalking the streets of Carlow as he would the surrounding terrain near his home in Woodfield outside Blessington, Co Wicklow where he now lived. While he was spotted that night of February 11 around 8 p.m. acting suspiciously, there is little doubt he had been in the area many times before, watching and waiting.

The object of his attention was a young businesswoman. As she got into her car, he approached her. Like a thief breaking into a house, he was in a high state of nervousness but that was just like an actor before walking on stage. And like the actor this brute had rehearsed the scenario many times in his mind and was ready. There was a risk and that added to the jingle-jangle of his nerves, but his compulsion was the master.

He smashed his fist into the face of the startled woman and pushed her into her own car, into the passenger seat. After ordering her to remove her bra, he tied her hands and feet. He then took the cash she had taken from her shop which amounted to almost €900.

This was a gratuitous action that made no sense. Murphy did not need the money but might have been trying to create the impression that the motive for the abduction was robbery. There could have been another reason. Many of his kind like to keep trophies taken from their victims, like clothes, jewellery or underwear. It provides further evidence of their power and a reference point to remember their actions.

Murphy then gagged the woman's mouth. His actions had taken no more than a minute and he moved with the speed and stealth of the practised hunter. He manoeuvred the car close to his own, which was parked nearby. He dragged her out of her car and practically lifted her to the rear of his own. He swung open the boot and in another swift movement had his intended victim locked into the tiny dark space. She felt the car speeding away. Murphy had carefully chosen to abduct this woman who was accomplished, strong of character, attractive and ran her own business successfully.

She represented everything that he detested in the opposite sex, confidence and self-assurance, which mocked all his real and perceived weaknesses. She was the sort of woman who did not seem vulnerable like others he might have attacked. He would enjoy all the more dominating her, humiliating her and teaching her who was really in control.

How smart and clever he thought himself to be. He had brought nothing into this abduction operation that could ever trace him to anything or anyone. Even in the height of his compulsion he was meticulous. Of course he had left traces in her car, fibres from his clothes, dirt from his boots and fingerprints. But that was academic and only of any value if there was a body. Without it there would be nothing with which to match any evidence.

But first he had to do this business he had dreamed about. It was not enough to kill the bitch. He was going to humiliate her and terrify the living daylights out of her. He drove on and later pulled up a boreen near a field. It was pitch black. The terrified woman was taken out of the boot and put in the passenger seat at the front of the car.

Murphy removed her clothes, indecently assaulted her and then proceeded to rape her violently. These acts had nothing to do with sex, per se, the rapist was exercising power and control. He made his victim kiss him, another meaningless response to an order. But by telling her afterwards that he was married with children she realised that it was the kiss of death.

She was then trussed up again and bundled back into the boot. Murphy got into the car and headed off for another destination. For all the woman in the boot knew, it was to be the site of her grave. She knew for certain, by the contours of the journey, that she was not going home ever. But Murphy was right about one thing. His victim was a strong woman who, during the course of the drive, tried to remember the direction of the twists and turns. She had not given up all hope despite the fact of knowing the ultimate intention of the rapist.

He stopped in a wooded area. The woman could hear the running water of a stream. He took her out of the boot again. She thought it might be the end. But he was not finished with his sickening lesson in sexual depravity, control and humiliation. This time the sexual order was that practised by the classical serial killer: violent vaginal rape followed by forced and highly painful anal sex and humiliating oral sex. The woman was cast in the role of sex slave, doing the degenerate master's bidding, the purpose of which was to inflict torture, suffering and pain.

He had rehearsed this scene many times during his masturbatory fantasies in which he used his penis as the instrument of ultimate power, defiling and degrading his imagined victim, punishing her for the power he perceived females had over him. But he was stronger and they were weaker and the rape and violence proved it beyond a shadow of doubt.

And yet the reality, as he now experienced it, was curiously unsatisfactory. He did not quite understand why. The greatest satisfaction had been in the chase and the tremendous high he got from anticipation. A curious depression fell on his mind, after the fact. He felt somehow worthless. In the life of his fantasies he was a different man, more powerful, more demanding, more punishing. In reality he felt weak and needed to communicate with his victim. A prelude to a violent death: a few words of self-pity. If he was found out he would never see his wife or children again. This was the jailer's tentative communication with the object of torture, to give him a slight air of humanity despite the appalling acts he had just perpetrated. He told the ravaged woman that life was not worth living. He placed, as his kind is wont to do, as little value on his own existence as on that of his victim's.

It is hardly conceivable that a man who has just carried out an appalling act of degradation should be pitching for pity from his victim. But this is the stuff such monsters are made of and yet one more notch in the character of the psycho killer. Pity me and give me the very obvious justification for killing. The shared intimacy of false feeling sends the message to the victim: this is why you must die. Such behaviour would seem to indicate that Larry Murphy had performed the ritual before.

He may have behaved like a monster, but he too was vulnerable. In the position he had adopted, that could not be allowed. He may think nothing of himself but not so little to let his victim go free. So he proceeded as planned. He shoved the woman back into the boot. With all her survival instincts she fought. He slammed the boot shut and returned with a plastic bag. The last act was about to begin.

He opened the boot and attempted to suffocate her with the bag. She fought like a demon and managed to get her feet over the rim of the boot. He shoved the bag into her mouth in a crude attempt to suffocate her and used all his considerable manic strength to cut off her airways. Just then the lights of an approaching Jeep illuminated the trees all around. Murphy went limp with fright. The killer had been caught in the act. The life of the young woman was saved.

But was it too late for others?

19
ONCE OFF – OR PART OF A PATTERN?

At the Central Criminal Court on May 11, 2002 Larry Murphy was jailed for fifteen years after pleading guilty to six charges of kidnapping, raping and attempted murder. Mr Justice Paul Carney also imposed further sentences on assault and robbery charges which, as usual, were to run concurrently. The final sentence in each case was suspended because of the guilty plea. That is the law and the judge, rightly, applied it to the letter. He could do no more or no less.

It was a justified and justifiable sentence. Nonetheless the implications are extremely worrying. Murphy, the meticulous carpenter, abductor and rapist, is equally likely to be as meticulous about his behaviour in prison, for a very good reason. With good behaviour this man can expect to serve two thirds of his sentence and by all accounts Murphy is a model prisoner.

He could therefore be free after eleven years by which time he will be far from geriatric status and, according to experts, will still represent a considerable danger to women. He does not talk to other prisoners about his crime or crimes and has not gone through any psychological rehabilitation programme. He has also refused to talk to detectives from the now defunct Operation Trace who would like to question him about the disappearances of Annie McCarrick, Jo Jo Dullard and Deirdre Jacob.

A person who refuses to talk, as any detective and journalist well knows, has something to hide. And Murphy, though facing a stiff sentence, clearly does not want to spend the rest of his life in prison. He felt no remorse for his victim and, had he killed previously, this attitude would not have changed. So why serve time for something that does not impinge on your conscience? His attitude is similar to that of Mark Nash though not to a long line of serial killers in other countries who admitted to many murders other than those they had been convicted of. In Ireland it seems closure for the families of the victims is not an issue.

It is a sobering thought that since the incarceration of John Crerar and Larry Murphy the abduction and murder of women in the east Leinster area has stopped – suddenly and without apparent explanation. There is one fact about such killers which is accepted as incontrovertible: they never stop of their own volition and if they do there is a reason – arrest and imprisonment, or death. If by any chance they change location, as Shaw and Evans did, it is to continue killing.

While Murphy has chosen to remain silent about whether he was involved in other murders he has, with the appalling crime he was convicted for, left a body of evidence in the method he employed to carry out the crime. The anatomy of his crime allows for a pathological examination on a behavioural and psychological level to determine whether Murphy was involved in the abduction and disappearances of other women in the areas he traversed while working as a roving carpenter.

In his excellent account of this case in his book, *Guilty: Violent Crimes in Ireland,* which covers a number of bizarre murders in this state, *Evening Herald* journalist, Stephen Rae, reveals a telling number of characteristics about Murphy. This provides material for a psychological analysis of Murphy's behaviour in relation to the behaviour of serial killers and raises great concern about any possible release for Murphy, however long in the future that may be.

Rae recounts that when a team of detectives led by Detective Sergeant James Ryan from Carlow and Sergeant Jack Kelleher from Tullow Station arrived at Murphy's house at 8.30 a.m. on the morning following the abduction, the suspect opened the door and let them in. After being cautioned, Murphy put his hands to his head and said, 'I don't know why it happened. I am terribly sorry.' When asked what he was doing in Carlow he replied that he was doing a house in Bennekebbery with his brother Tom. 'Why did I do that?' he remarked.

After informing his wife the reason why the gardaí were present, he asked if he could go to the bathroom to comb his hair. Accompanied by a member of the unit, he looked in the mirror and said, 'Why did I do it?'

At no stage did he express remorse or concern for the victim's state of physical and mental health. During questioning he appeared sullen and dour again with no hint of conscience. A man with a half-way normal emotional make-up would have been racked with guilt and regret for his actions and expressed concern for the victim, particularly if this was the first time he had carried out such a crime: a young woman brutally attacked and violated sexually in the most abominable manner then marked out for suffocation and strangulation, her body to be buried without trace.

The implications of his brutality seemed not to impinge on Murphy in the slightest way. This marks him out as an incredibly rare species of killer. In the geographical area where he lives and works he is matched only by John Crerar.

These men according to the best research on the subject carried out in Britain and the United States represent one in a million of the population. And they operated in a tiny geographical triangle, which includes Kildare, Kilkenny, Carlow and Wicklow. The statistical possibility, according to experts, of anyone else of similar inclination and behaviour operating in that tiny triangle is about the same as winning the Lottery.

Murphy claimed that he committed the crime on impulse. He said that when he saw the girl, he just flipped. When questioned why he had put the woman in his own car and driven off he remarked about the action: 'I don't know why I did.' This reaction has an exact echo with Mark Nash's explanation for his murderous behaviour.

This, as experts attest, is a blatant lie to give the impression that the motivation for the abduction was in some way random. But his lack of remorse is a truth. Studies of the basic psychology of pyscho killers along with their own testimony consistently arrive at one conclusion: the absence of remorse kicks in with the repetition of sex killing. In 99% of these killers the first crime produces fear, revulsion and remorse. Even Ted Bundy, one of America's most prolific and notorious serial killers, expressed horror and remorse after his first planned attack on a potential victim. He was a voyeur and liked to watch young women undress. One evening in the summer of 1973 while drinking heavily Bundy spotted a woman leave a bar and walk up a dark side street. He followed her and found a piece of wood in a vacant parking lot and stalked her. He got ahead of the girl and lay in wait but before she reached the point where he was, she turned and went into a house.

Bundy later described himself as horrified by the recognition that he had the capacity to harm another individual. He said he was seized with disgust, repulsion and fear at why he was allowing himself to attempt such extraordinary violence. But his compulsion was too great and he went on to murder over twenty-nine women. After the first two or three murders, the remorse and revulsion were replaced by an addiction. Bundy like most serial killers could not stop.

Significantly the random nature of Bundy's first experience was replaced by stalking and planned abduction. This pattern is often compared to a progressive disease. Larry Murphy displayed symptoms that prove he was suffering the later stages of that 'illness'. Lack of remorse was just one but there were others.

During questioning Murphy admitted to a number of other sexual assaults and rapes. One rape had taken place close to Moone where Jo Jo Dullard disappeared. These assaults and rapes are often the initial steps along with voyeurism on the road to serial killing. And those crimes are not motivated by sexual needs but by the desire to exercise power and control over the victims.

There is a sense of power to be drawn by Peeping Tom and stalking activities. This is gained from observing a woman who does not know she is being watched and then having masturbatory fantasies in which that power over her is rehearsed in the mind. These fantasies are predominantly founded on violence as opposed to sex, in which the 'object' is subjected to torture and humiliation.

It is instructive to know something of the nature of those

fantasies to get an insight into the awful depths of minds of men like Larry Murphy. The violence of the fantasies is often in direct proportion to the extent of sexual dysfunction in the individual. The more marked the premature ejaculation or inability to attain and maintain the erection, the more violent the fantasy.

In the fantasies the woman is typically impaled on a penis which is the implement of torture and punishment as well as other objects such as knives or swords. These are employed to cut the nipples and breasts, to insert into the vagina, and to titillate and then cut out the clitoris. Other objects such as bottles and brush handles are inserted in the vagina and anus.

The female is typically tied hand and foot while these rituals are enacted and they scream with both pleasure and pain. They are then strangled either manually or with their tights or bras. The fantasist can sometimes only climax at the point of the fantasy object's death during the act of strangulation.

Violent anal rape and forced oral sex is the mainstay of many of these fantasists because it is a brutal and direct method of inflicting pain. The fantasist sometimes brings another man into the sadistic sex acts to double the pain. Curiously the fantasists imagine that the female objects reach states of ecstasy by being subjected to these practices.

An undercover operation in the UK encouraged the prime suspect of a sex killing to put his fantasies on paper to a female policewoman. In each one a knife is employed in scenarios such as this:

> I go between your legs and fuck you hard again. You
> are now impaled at both ends by two swollen cocks. As

> I fuck you I draw the knife around your neck. Drops
> of blood splatter the man's naked legs. You're now
> screaming in ecstasy. His cock springs from your
> mouth and you lap up the blood, at the same time he
> is wanking into your hair and face.

During the investigation of a similar suspect in Ireland he put down
on paper the real account of a fantasy translated into the reality of
anal rape.

> She's a dirty old hag so I decided to fuck her up the
> arse, so I don't have to look at her face. When I shoved
> it up the first time, she cried with pain and said it hurt.
> I told her to shut up because she had no fucking
> choice. The second time she cried and said it hurt. But
> she had no fucking choice. It was the same the third
> and fourth time. She did not complain after that
> because she knew she had no fucking choice.

The next stage is to move from fantasy to reality through the
medium of sexual assault and rape, and then murder and the
development of an appetite that becomes insatiable.

Ted Bundy's account of the movement from stage two to three is
remarkable for the simple fact of how quickly it happened and how
the compulsion increased. Bundy moved from the peeping Tom
stage to creeping into a basement after he had watched a girl
undressing. He took a metal bar from the bed frame and hit her
over the head. Then finding himself unable to get an erection, he
rammed the metal bar up her vagina. He then fled. The girl

subsequently recovered and for the next month Bundy wrestled with his demons, full of remorse and self-disgust.

Then he made it to the next stage. Breaking into student lodging rooms, he came upon a young student Lynda Ann Healy whom he abducted, bound and gagged. He then put her in the boot of his car and drove twenty miles to a mountainous area outside Seattle where he subjected her to six hours of vile sexual sadism. He finally bludgeoned her to death and left her body on the mountain.

Lynda Ann Healy was the first of four women he raped and murdered in the same place. The similarity of Bundy's first abduction with the Larry Murphy case is chilling and prompts one to wonder if Murphy had brought other women to that remote mountainous spot in Wicklow.

These crimes are in essence motivated by the need for violation and violence spurred by feelings of inadequacy, unreasoned hatred and the overwhelming desire to dominate women by force. The ultimate power for these men, say analysts, is murder. The next stage. Both experts consulted on this case agree that when Larry Murphy abducted the young woman in Carlow both his actions on the night and his mental demeanour during questioning suggested that he had already progressed to that stage.

While Murphy did not say much, what he did say was highly significant in both determining his category of sex killer and establishing whether he had killed before.

A forensic psychiatrist analysing Murphy's remarks and backed up by an experienced murder investigator concludes that they come from a man who is a practised liar with no hint of responsibility or remorse for his crime. His remarks expressing confusion at his actions contradict the facts of the abduction and rape: it was planned and executed with murderous intent. There were no questions in his mind about his actions. His concern is totally for himself; he tells his wife of his predicament with absolutely no feeling for her or his children.

Most revealing of all was during his interrogation when it was put to him that his victim was going through a lot in the aftermath of what he had done. Murphy's reply was, 'Well she is alive, isn't she?'

His reaction to the arrival of the investigation team is in itself calculated. He knew that the victim would have been brought by the hunters to Baltinglass Police Station and given a statement and that more than likely he had been identified by the men in the Jeep. And yet he tries to give the impression that he did not know what drove him to do what he did. This was calculated to absolve him from some blame by giving the false impression that there was no intent involved. In other words, he had been seized by a sudden crazy impulse and in some way was out of control and therefore had diminished responsibility for his actions. This of course was a calculated lie, underlined by the narcissism that typifies such killers. He has just been arrested for a sexually sadistic crime of horrific proportions and he asks to go to the toilet to comb his hair. And there he plays the role of the mystified criminal, combing away and wondering aloud, 'Why did I do it?'

He is trying to give the impression that what he did was the action of a reckless risk taker. That may well have been the case earlier in his life when indulging in sexual assaults and rapes, crimes which he admitted to investigators. But men of his psychotic type tend to get more cautious and wise as they mature. In other words, what they might have done on impulse when younger is now planned and worked out. Instead of just randomly picking up a girl and raping her, there will be a stalking process before striking.

There is also a process of selection of the victim, which is chillingly illustrated by a case history going back to the forties in America. On the evening of April 22, 1942 a pretty seventeen-year-old named Alice Porter was walking home from a nursing class in Pueblo, Colorado. A car pulled up beside her and she was bundled in. A neighbour heard the girl scream and looked out in time to see a light-coloured Ford sedan disappearing down the street.

The girl was driven to a one-roomed ranch building twenty-five miles away and there was raped and tortured for six hours. She was bound with red-hot wires and stabbed with an awl. Then she was hit with a hammer and shot twice through the head. Her body was concealed in a cistern.

Three days later investigators located a garage owner who had been woken up at 4 a.m. to tow a light-coloured Ford Sedan out of the mud the day after Alice Porter's disappearance. Investigators went to the location and found the abandoned ranch at the top of a nearby hill. A search inside revealed bloodstains and instruments of torture including an awl. In the cistern they discovered the body of Alice Porter.

Fingerprints were lifted from the awl but there was no match in the records of criminal offenders. Officers searched garages looking for any sighting of the Ford Sedan and then found it, waiting its turn to be washed. When the owner returned to his car he was arrested. Donald Fearn a twenty-three-year-old mechanic was taken in for questioning and his fingerprints matched those on the awl.

Fearn admitted that he had fantasies about torturing a girl and he had waited in his car outside the building where nursing classes took place for weeks, following different students home. Finally he chose Alice Porter as his victim. The perpetrator was later executed.

The case resonates with Murphy in that it demonstrates that the selection and pursuit of a victim by the sexual sadist, far from being random, is carefully thought out in advance. Both Murphy and Fearn had a clear image of the type of woman they wanted to violate.

Murphy was in his mid-thirties at the time of the abduction and there is definite eyewitness evidence that he was lurking in the vicinity of the victim's shop for some time before he made his initial move. That clearly establishes his modus operandi. He has his impulse under control. He has no doubt in his mind about what he is going to do. He has become a calculated risk assessor and self-preservation is very important to him.

That sense of self-preservation was underpinned by the fact that in the mainstream of his life he had a lot to lose. Unlike psychotics like Mark Nash, Vinnie Connell and Shaw and Evans who constantly made a mess of their lives and perceived that they had nothing to lose by their monstrous behaviour, Murphy was a good tradesman and was doing well. He was married and his life was measured with no hint of chaos except in the presence of, and interaction with, the opposite sex. We might well ask where the aberrant mind fits in with the things that make Larry Murphy indistinguishable from any other married man with steady employment.

The fact is that he knew well why he did what he did and that every phase of the abduction and rape had been planned like a military exercise. The real clue to assessing whether Larry Murphy had abducted before lies not just simply in the apparent coincidence that he was working in Roseberry the day that Deirdre Jacob disappeared but an examination of his mind, behaviour and the mechanics of the abduction of the young Carlow businesswoman.

There is little on the surface in what is known of Murphy's background to indicate the genesis of the monster he became. He was one of seven children brought up in a small Wicklow village and was not of academic inclination. What he did excel at was woodwork, which was noted and appreciated at the vocational school he attended and which he left at sixteen years of age. He became in time an accomplished carpenter and despite his academic limitations proved that he would have no problem earning a living.

The lack of academic qualifications does not mean that Murphy lacks intelligence. Very often the reverse is true. Research shows that killers tend to have a high intelligence and to be organised and methodical. They plan their crimes in detail and exert greater control over their victims. The abduction of the Carlow woman puts the perpetrator firmly into this category. By any manner or means, Larry Murphy is no fool. He differs from killers like Ted Bundy in that he refuses to say whether he was involved in the disappearances of other women. Then again Bundy was facing execution as were Smith and Hickock. They had nothing to gain by hiding their actions and motives. Murphy has everything to lose with the knowledge that in a relatively short time, he will be free.

Mark Nash has taken the same option as Murphy. Despite the fact that these men should never, given the seriousness of their actions, be given the opportunity to repeat their crimes, they will both one day be free.

Notwithstanding Murphy's assured social status he clearly had no sense of value of his achievements. The rewards of his labour did nothing to neutralise his pervasive sense of low self-esteem. One thing he said to his victim had the ring of truth and confirmed this poor view of himself: life, he said, was not worth living.

This might appear to be a blatant contradiction to the facts of his existence but in reality it exposed the highly charged and dangerous state of his mind. All the more so because it was *his* truth.

For some reason, despite the relative success of his life, he felt powerless and impotent. The obliteration of that powerless state came in the form of his chaotic entrance into the world of sexual sadism and murder. The brutal enactment of his fantasy life. The construction of power from the foundation of weakness.

The fact that Murphy was clearly unhappy with the reality of his life indicated that he withdrew more and more into the world of fantasy where he could realise what he perceived was his full potential. Long sessions of erotic daydreaming will pump up a flagging ego which has in all likelihood been dented by some sexual dysfunction such as difficulty in attaining an erection or premature ejaculation. The predominant theme of Murphy's sexual fantasies involve the sadistic punishment of his sex slave.

This is the classic Jekyll and Hyde syndrome. On the outside this man is a respectable family man but inside his head there is a monster waiting to take over the outside persona. There is a muddled quest for the fulfilment lacking in his life. In the absence of this fulfilment he can be subject to depressive and sometimes suicidal thoughts. For much the same reason as anyone else, the thought is that if life means nothing now, the chances are that it never will.

In the history of such sex and lust killers he is not alone. And it must be remembered that, in his case, he was convicted of attempted murder. It was proved and he admitted the intention to kill his victim. The fact that he tried to suffocate the young woman whom he had subjected to appalling violence and rape consigned this intent beyond any reasonable doubt in a court.

His confession to the woman that life is not worth living is both evidence of his psychotic tendencies and worthy of comparison to others of his inclination to illustrate just how dangerous they are. While Murphy said little to his interrogators what he did say is a revelation of the constant state of his mind. A state that experts says will never change.

Murphy has, in many newspaper reports and Stephen Rae's account in his book, been described as a loner, someone who operated outside the usual social norms, another classical feature that links him to men who have carried out the sort of crime he was convicted of. In a forensic psychiatrist's evaluation these type of men think as little of themselves as they do of their victim. Albert Brust was such a man.

In July 1973 a housewife in South Dade County, Florida was in her garden when she noticed that her next-door neighbour Albert Brust was sitting in his chair, staring into space without noticing the rain. When her son told her that he had been in that same position for two days, she rang the police.

A postmortem revealed that he had died from self-administered cyanide poisoning. While the police were searching the house, they were overpowered by a foul smell. They traced it to the bathroom where behind the shower curtain was a newly constructed concrete wall. From a corner there was blood seeping.

The wall was pulled down to reveal a headless corpse which had been extensively mutilated. As the police went through the rooms, it proved to be a house of horrors with an array of implements of torture, an extensive library of pornography and obscene pictures. Brust, a forty-four-year-old buildings inspector, had spent time in prison some two decades before where he had become expert at carpentry and welding. He went on to work in the construction industry before being appointed a buildings inspector. He was a loner with very few friends. He drove a motorcycle and sometimes confided in the owner of a local motorcycle shop. His conversations were dominated with talk of sex, suicide and murder. He was solitary, depressive and self-obsessed and put down his morbid thoughts in a diary. Like Bundy's confessions and admissions, the diary provided a unique insight into the mind of a man whose inclination is to abduct, rape, torture and murder.

According to the motorcycle shop owner he was consumed with deep angst and a hatred for almost everything. He was only interested in a relationship with women that involved their being sex slaves. 'I need someone for sex,' he wrote in his diary, 'but not an idiot I have to cater to.'

His solution was to kidnap a young couple who were hitchhiking and bring them back to the house of horrors where he forced Mark

Matson and Mary Ellen Jones to perform a number of sex acts. Mark tried to overcome Brust but Brust was too quick and shot him, killing him. Brust dragged the body into the bathroom and then took the girl to his torture chamber where he shackled her to the wall and raped her repeatedly over the next twenty-four hours.

Like Larry Murphy's victim, Mary Ellen expected to die but Brust drove her to Fort Lauderdale and released her. She went to the police. When they contacted her mother, she claimed that her daughter was a persistent liar and so the matter was not investigated. The fact that Brust released her could only mean one thing, that he intended to end it all which he did just five days after the abduction. The final entry in his diary exposed his state of mind.

> I have miscalculated. I know I can save the situation
> by a lot of disagreeable work but I see no good reason
> for going on. What would come next? The whole
> business is not worth it; life is not worth the trouble
> after all.

Albert Brust's last words have an exact resonance with Murphy's remarks to his victim. Murphy's statement also reveals that despite the capture, rape and the sexual sadism, Murphy felt a sense of anticlimax. It was as if the reality, when achieved, still did not match the fantasy. Or was it that the thrill of the hunt meant everything? The expert hunter, he had yet another counterpart in pyscho killing history, a case which may reveal something more of Murphy's nature.

20
THE HUNTER IN THE WOODS

An aviation map in the attic of successful businessman Robert Hansen had twenty asterisks covering a large area outside the town of Anchorage in Alaska. The markings indicated the approximate location of shallow graves in which a dangerous killer had buried his victims. Whether the map represented a boastful body count or allowed the killer to return to the scene of the crime was not clear. Either way it provided evidence against a man who was convinced that he would never be caught and that the remains of his victims would melt into the remote landscape where they had been buried.

In the seventies and early eighties a number of dancers from Anchorage strip clubs disappeared. At first the disappearances did not arouse too much suspicion: women working in strip clubs come and go at the drop of a hat. But when the women did not appear to collect their wages, the club owners were puzzled. That was completely out of character.

In 1980 building workers came across the body of a woman whose grave had been disturbed by hungry bears and the body half-eaten. The state of the corpse made identification impossible. Hunters found another grave two years later just outside Anchorage. It was that of a dancer who had disappeared almost a year previously. She had been shot three times and ballistics established that she had been murdered by a high-velocity hunting rifle.

As there were hundreds of such guns in use in the area this clue lead nowhere. One year later another grave was found not far from the second and it was established that this was occupied by the body of another dancer who had gone missing. It was that of Paula Golding who had, because of shortage of work, started working in a topless bar. Eight days after starting work in April 1983, she had gone missing, leaving her wages uncollected. Clearly she had been abducted and murdered.

Even though there were bodies, there were no clues to the identity of the killer. Investigators often need a lucky break to open up an avenue and the previous June something happened that made things a bit clearer. A policeman had come across a teenage prostitute running along a street crying out for help. She described being picked up by an ugly red-haired man with pock-marked skin and a stutter who had solicited her for oral sex. She had accompanied him back to his house in a well-appointed suburb of Anchorage. He took her to the basement, ordered her to remove her clothes and shackled her to a pillar. He then subjected her to a routine of sadistic sexual practices including shoving a hammer handle up her vagina, a practice shared by Ted Bundy and other sex killers. It is their method of inflicting punishment on women at times when they experience impotence.

It was when he was taking her to his small private plane that she made her escape. Police deduced from this story that the suspect was Robert Hansen a successful baker and this was confirmed when the prostitute identified his as the house she had been taken to. However when confronted Hansen said that he had a cast-iron alibi from two business acquaintances.

It was the very same sort of alibi secured from colleagues by John Crerar – false. But with the discovery of Paula Golding's body the investigators returned to Hansen via his business friends whom they reminded that lying under oath can bring a two-year prison sentence. They admitted that they had provided the alibi at Hansen's request and that they had not been in his company that night.

Hansen was charged with abduction and rape, and the investigators secured a search warrant for his house. There they found the aviation map and a number of items of women's jewellery. At least two of the asterisks marked locations where bodies had already been found. Hansen at first denied everything but then relented and confessed. He also confessed to other abductions and murders, which, unlike in this country, meant that he would get consecutive sentences amounting to 461 years.

But more telling than his confessions was his explanation of the motivation for the crimes. Despite his success in life, he could not shake off the low self-esteem that had been bred in his youth where his ugliness and acne made him a target of fun and rejection by the girls. His abiding fantasy was of a docile girl performing oral sex.

He found plenty of opportunity to indulge his fantasies with the plethora of strip joints and topless bars in Anchorage, most of them a legitimate front for prostitution. If the girls did not want to fellate him, then he produced a gun.

Hansen was a top-class hunter and his thrill was in the chase with the kill being an anticlimax. He began to fantasise what it would be like to replace the animals with females. He would pick up a prostitute and if she performed oral sex satisfactorily, he would drive her back to Anchorage. If not, he would bring her to the wilds, hunt her down as she fled naked, shoot her and bury her in a grave. Each grave then became an asterisk on his map.

Hansen had become the ultimate hunter of women, revelling in the sheer power he could exercise over them and feasting like a vampire on the terror and suffering his victims experienced in their last moments. Just like Larry Murphy.

The abduction during which Murphy was caught, the forensic psychiatrist and investigator suggest, was not the nadir of his involvement in such acts. Most sexual attacks are carried out by young men and there is little doubt in the minds of the experts that at the time of his arrest, Larry Murphy was well-practised in that activity, a fact he admitted under questionning. An examination of the abduction and rape showed strong parallels with other documented cases where the perpetrator had progressed some time before to killing his victims.

Can anything else adequately explain why, after he was caught in the act that fateful night, the abduction and murder of young women in territory that he traversed and with which he was familiar suddenly stopped?

As one profiler put it:

> A man does not wake up one morning and become a sexual psychopath nor does he wake up one day and it is gone. It has developed over a very long time and does not go away, in nearly all cases, until the perpetrator is caught. This is our experience of such killers all over the world.

In his opinion sexual psychopaths will always pose a danger to women and there should be no limit applied to the period of their incarceration.

21
COMPOSITE KILLER – THE PROFILE

Despite the different circumstances of the killings and abductions dealt with so far, whether solved or unsolved, there is a composite picture that can be drawn of the sort of killer who stoops to the depths of depravity that involves the violation and ultimate destruction of, in the majority of cases, young women. Young women enthused and hopeful for the future and ready for the ordinary challenges that life has to offer. Until they come into the clutches of a killer who feasts on them in an orgy of sex and violence and then without a second thought snuffs out the lights of their lives leaving their loved ones to suffer an unrelenting nightmare until they rest in the finality and peace of their own graves.

That suffering should not be underestimated, for the killer does not just kill his victim but also a family. It is a crime that cries out for appropriate punishment often not available in our courts.

It is an unfortunate fact that in Ireland this type of killer is not the subject of studies which could provide information for forensic psychiatrists and murder investigators to help prevent or quickly solve crimes. While the art of profiling is by no means an exact science the process is being continually refined to help build up a mental map of the killer, just as a forensic artist produces a physical photo-fit.

There are a number of sources from which highly accurate assumptions can be drawn. These include postmortem reports and photographs, which illustrate the manner and ferocity of the attack, the position of the body and, in crimes involving sex, how and when semen was deposited, what other parts of the anatomy were interfered with and whether the interference took place before or after death.

Other information can be gleaned from a study of transcripts of interviews with suspects, the crime scene, conversations with members of the investigating team and, if the victim had been abducted or the body moved, possible connections between the location and the perpetrator.

Specific injuries to the body can further add to the portrait of the killer. If the victim has been subjected to humiliation and torture, the deviant nature of the attacker can be assessed, whether he works in manual employment or an office environment, and what age category he falls into. As well as such factors, educated guesswork and intuition come into play.

Top profilers not only utilise the facts available to them but can put themselves into the minds of the killers and see the world through their eyes. The identity of many perpetrators of serious crime, from murder, rape, abduction and kidnapping, have been established with the help of profilers. They have, by narrowing the focus of investigation, not only helped to convict those responsible for the crimes but also saved police authorities a huge amount of time and money.

While profiling is not new it has been developed to be an art in the US and Britain because crime-fighting authorities believe in its intrinsic value. Not so in Ireland, unfortunately, because the expertise requires, as in the matter of the missing, more respect and more resources. If the profile of the Grangegorman killer had been taken seriously enough, the murderer might now be convicted. The profile of Raonaid Murray's killer is also a model of its kind, a model that goes back a long time to demonstrate that the innate character of killers of this kind does not change.

The model was provided by Dr Joseph Satten of the Meninger Clinic in Topeka, Kansas mentioned earlier in relation to his agreement with Dr Jones's assessment of Dick Hickock and Perry Smith in the Clutter murders. His article *Murder Without Apparent Motive* published in 1960 is classic and his examination of four convicted murderers provides profiles which could fit killers in Ireland decades later. Dr Satten found:

> Despite the violence in their lives, all the men had ego images of themselves as inferior, weak and inadequate. Their histories revealed that in each case there was a degree of sexual inhibition. To all of them adult women were threatening creatures and in two there was overt sexual perversion. In four there was evidence of altered states of consciousness, frequently in connection with outbreaks of violence.
>
> Two men reported severe disassociative trance-like states during which violent and bizarre behaviour was seen, while the other two reported less severe and perhaps less well-organised amnesiac states. During moments of violence they often felt separated or isolated from themselves as if they were watching somebody else . . . there was a common experience of violence at the hands of family in their youth.

The history relating to *extreme* violence, whether fantasised, observed in reality or actually experienced by the child, fits in with the psychoanalytic hypothesis that the child's exposure to overwhelming stimuli, before he can master them, is closely linked to early defects in ego formation and, later, severe disturbances in impulse control.

In all cases there was evidence of severe emotional deprivation in early life. This deprivation may have involved prolonged or recurrent absence of one or both parents, with the child being reared by others. None reported feelings of rage in association with the murders although each was capable of enormous and brutal aggression. Their relationships with others were of a shallow nature and their emotions in relation to murders and their own fate was also shallow. Guilt and remorse were strikingly absent.

Such individuals can be considered murder-prone in the sense of carrying a surcharge of excess energy or having an unstable ego defence system that allows a naked and archaic expression of such energy. The murderous potential can become activated, especially if some dis-equilibrium is present and the victim is to be unconsciously perceived in some past traumatic configuration. The behaviour, or even mere presence, of this figure adds a stress to the unstable balance of forces that results in a sudden extreme violence that takes place when a percussion cap ignites a charge of dynamite.

The hypothesis of unconscious motivation explains why the murderers perceived relatively unknown victims as suitable targets of aggression. But why murder? Most people, fortunately, do not respond with murderous outbursts even under extreme provocation. The case studies were predisposed to gross lapses in reality contact and extreme weakness in impulse control during periods of heightened tension and disorganisation.

When such senseless murders occur, they are often seen to be an end result of a period of increasing tension and disorganisation. At such times a chance acquaintance or even a stranger was able to lose her or his 'real' meaning. The victim, by fitting into the unconscious conflicts of the murderer, unwittingly serves to set into motion his homicidal pattern.

Dr Satten and other psychiatrists who studied the mentality of such killers over the years and decades noted that they have an explosive, self-pitying reaction to rejection which the majority of people take in their stride. This can be attributed to the fact that the former have personalities of a childish and undisciplined nature, and rejection tears apart the foundation of insecure self-esteem.

A complementary reaction is the desire for power and control that the killer does not have in his own life but which he wants to impose on someone else to boost his self-esteem. This 'control freak' syndrome operates a regime of total obedience at home. If his instructions are not followed to the letter, at home or in work, he is liable to fly into a rage.

The search is for some form of self-esteem that is pathologically lacking in their background and mentality. Behavioural analysts have categorised this aspect to their character and their crimes are, among other motivations, a desire for recognition even if that is achieved by rape and murder. Ironically, many of these type could have achieved, given their intellect, high places in their chosen professions, had the evil side of their personas not come to the fore.

Mad or bad is the next question to apply to the type of killer with which we have dealt. A question for which there is no easy answer.

The question was asked most pertinently as far back as 1601 when William Shakespeare completed *Hamlet*, his most popular and voluminously discussed play. To this day, the question whether the main character was mad or was merely acting mad has inspired millions of words, debates and theories. What is not at issue is the fact that the play ends in a bloodbath of which Hamlet is both the inspiration and the architect.

Hamlet describes himself as a man crawling between heaven and earth and as an arrant knave, not to be believed. He is on a trail of murder and mayhem no different to the infamous and brilliant Ted Bundy, and as equally trapped by self-delusion.

Hamlet is not mad, he is bad, self-pitying and grossly self-centred, a spoilt, unhinged and dangerous brat, who wants his own way, at any cost. In simple psychological terms, he is infused with the desire to behave like a spoilt brat and to punish those who do not do what the child demands.

In *The Serial Killers*, subtitled *A Study in the Psychology of*

Violence, Colin Wilson and Donald Seaman sum up this attitude brilliantly captured by Shakespeare, nearly four centuries later:

> It is easy to understand the development of the syndrome. There is nobody in the world who does not want his own way. Most of us learn to make realistic adjustments to not getting our own way. This is obviously easier for someone whose life is fairly stable. Children with serious problems – difficult parents, broken homes, traumatic frustrations – tend to react to disappointments with an out of proportion sense of misery and defeat.

> They compensate by fantasy, and perhaps (like Bundy) by lying and stealing. These reactions have an identical root; both are attempts to take what the world refuses to give freely. If this 'naughty boy' aspect goes unpunished (as with Bundy) it can develop into a kind of self-indulgence that strikes us as insane, but which is actually a calculated and conscious form of wickedness.

There is little doubt that this is the truth in relation to the killers dealt with in this book. Mark Nash, John Crerar, John Shaw and Geoffrey Evans, Vinnie Connell and Larry Murphy represent the very epitome of cruel, self-indulgent evil. As does the killer of Raonaid Murray. There are exceptions to the rule. The late Brendan O'Donnell who murdered Imelda Riney, her son Liam and Fr Joe Walshe was clinically insane and there are others who are similarly incarcerated in the Central Mental Hospital in Dundrum.

Despite the cessation in the disappearances of women there is little reason to be complacent at a time in this country when they are increasingly targets for violence of all kinds: assault, rape and murder. Unfortunately it seems that psychopaths who wreak much of this damage will always be with us. It is up to the authorities to protect its citizens but there is very little appetite for that on the part of the Government.

Clearly from the evidence of the long campaign mounted by John McGuinness TD and Mary Phelan nothing has changed since the disappearance of Jo Jo Dullard and Deirdre Jacob. Missing persons and victims are very low on the list of priorities of the Department of Justice unless politics is involved. How quickly would the Department order a dig for the bodies of Jo Jo Dullard and Deirdre Jacob as opposed to the bodies of victims of IRA death squads?

It has to be remembered that the murder victims were people with ambitions, hopes and aspirations, cruelly obliterated by evil men. They should never be mere numbers, either in the public or private arenas. The families, especially those of the disappeared, have been condemned to a lifetime of misery by the killers. Our outmoded and outdated system of justice will ensure that those who pose a horrendous danger to women and the public will not be given a life sentence in its true meaning.

The sooner we introduce consecutive sentencing in the US manner, the better we can protect our society against psychos like Nash, Crerar and Murphy. The sooner we recognise the huge importance of profiling, the better we can hunt such men down. In the movingly humane conclusion of his book, *The Jigsaw Man*, one of Britain's top profilers Paul Britton, who has worked on over 100 murder cases, writes:

> Looking back I don't remember the victims' faces because usually the pictures I see are taken after death when the light has gone out of their eyes. What I do remember are their minds because so much of what I do involves learning the intimate details and rhythm of their lives. It's knowing them and what happened to them that makes the pain and sadness of their deaths even greater.
>
> The memories will never go away and they are the most potent reason why I can't say no when the police call. Each time I see the minds, hundreds of them, a sea of people who have been raped, murdered, abused and damaged; and somewhere there is a man who will continue to hurt. He's likely to be sitting and remembering what he did, savouring it and gaining sexual pleasure from recounting it. He's real, he's out there and eventually his urge will begin to build up again. I can't always predict when this will happen but I do know that unless he is stopped he is going to kill again and again.

We need more men like Paul Britton if we are to deal adequately with the phenomenon of psycho killing in Ireland. In his well-informed opinion it is not simply going to go away. History, here and in other countries, has proved him right.

BIBLIOGRAPHY

In Cold Blood, Truman Capote. Penguin Classics (2002)

Dead Reckoning: The New Science of Catching Killers Dr Michael Baden and Marion Roach. Arrow Books (2002)

The Serial Killer: A Study in the Psychology of Violence Colin Wilson and Donald Seaman. Virgin Books (2001)

Autumn of Terror Tom Cullen. Bodley Head (1965)

Jack the Ripper: The Final Solution Stephen Knight. HarperCollins (1975)

Portrait of a Killer: Jack the Ripper – Case Closed Patricia Cornwell. Little, Brown (2002)

Killing for Company: The Story of a Man Addicted to Murder Brian Masters. Jonathan Cape (1985)

The Want-Ad Killer Anne Rule. Penguin (2003)

The Jigsaw Man: The Remarkable Career of Britain's Foremost Criminal Psychologist Paul Britton. Corgi (1998)

Guilty: Violent Crimes in Ireland Stephen Rae. Blackwater Press (2002)

Missing: Missing Without Trace in Ireland Barry Cummins. Gill and Macmillan (2003)